"Vibrant Future" International Education Project for Young Artists

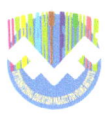

VIBRANT VISIONS
International Youth Artist Artwork Series-5

Artists: Elaine V. Kuang, Jiajun Deng, Ziyan Chen, Rong Hong, Lulia Gao, Yuiyan Wan, Xiyu Zhang, Yihan Hu, Emma Chen
Editor-in-Chief: Yemen Chen
Deputy Editor-in-Chief: Jia Zhong
Editors: Elaine V. Kuang, Jiajun Deng
Cover designer: Jiajun Deng
Book designer: Jiajun Deng
Cover Artwork by: Ziyan Chen

Losget Press
International Society of Young Artists
2024

International Youth Artist Artwork Series-5

"Vibrant Future"
International Education
Project for Young Artists

Artists: Elaine V. Kuang, Jiajun Deng, Ziyan Chen, Rong Hong, Lujia Gao, Yuiyan Wan, Xiyu Zhang, Yihan Hu, Emma Chen
Editor-in-Chief: Yemen Chen
Deputy Editor-in-Chief: Jia Zhong
Editors: Elaine V. Kuang, Jiajun Deng
Cover designer: Jiajun Deng
Book designer: Jiajun Deng
Cover Artwork by: Ziyan Chen

 Copyright © 2024 by International Society of Young Artists
All rights reserved.

LOSGET Published in the United States by Losget Press, Los Angeles.
Originally published in paperback in the United States by Losget Press, in 2024.
Library of Congress Cataloging-in-Publication Data
Names: Kuang, Elaine V./ Deng, Jiajun/ Chen, Ziyan/ Hong, Rong/ Gao, Lujia/ Wan, Yuiyan/ Hu, Yihan/ Chen, Emma, authors.
Title: Vibrant Visions: International Youth Artist Artwork Series-5
Description: First edition. | Los Angeles: Losget Press, 2024.
Identifiers: LCCN: 2024915884/ ISBN: 978-1-951364-40-3
E-mail: losgetpress@gmail.com
First printing. 2024.

Foreword

The International Society of Young Artists (ISOYA) is a non-profit organization associated with Losget Academy. Founded in Los Angeles in 2019, ISOYA has quickly evolved into a vibrant community of talented young artists united by their passion for creativity and self-expression.

That same year, ISOYA launched the "Vibrant Future" International Education Project for Young Artists. This program is committed to providing world-class artistic education to young people globally. To date, it has fostered the creation of 14 individual art portfolio books and the remarkable collective art book, "International Artist Artwork Series." This initiative has significantly contributed to many ISOYA members securing places at some of the world's premier art schools and universities.

"Vibrant Visions: International Youth Artist Artwork Series-5" showcases a stunning collection of visual pieces from nine gifted teenage artists. These works vividly capture the bright colors and radiant energy of their youthful essence, providing a window into their innovative spirits.

We envision each young artist's potential as a seed of artistic expression, destined to bloom into a dazzling array of brilliant creations. Fueled by the rich soil of education and nurtured by the invigorating dew of inspiration, these emerging talents are poised to produce the finest fruits of the art world.

Yemen Chen
President of the International Society of Young Artists
January 2024

The Liberty Awards

Awarded for outstanding achievements in the field of art by young American and international artists, the award is presented by the International Society of Young Artists. It was first awarded in 2018.

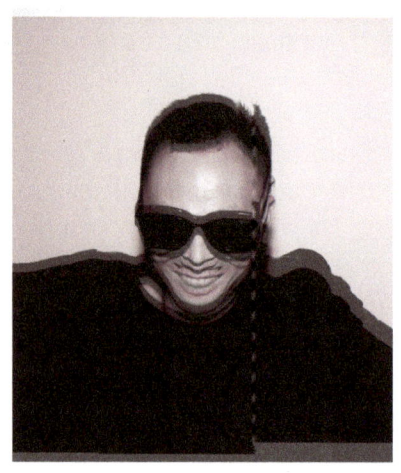

YEMEN CHEN, Jury Chair
Artist/ Litterateur/ Songwriter/ Music Producer/ President of the International Society of Young Artists
His 3 art books and 7 literary books have been published, and he has created and produced over 20 music albums. Additionally, he has served as the editor-in-chief for more than 20 books. One of his philosophical works was included in the Gaokao examination paper.
MAJOR ART BOOKS: *East 100*, *Illusion*.
MAJOR LITERATURE BOOKS: *Skeleton Garden*, *Michelangelo DiCaprio*, *Book of Chinese Homophones*, *Book of Chinese Full-Rhymes*, *Book of Chinese Alliterations*.
MAJOR MUSIC ALBUMS: *Vincent van Gogh*, *America*.

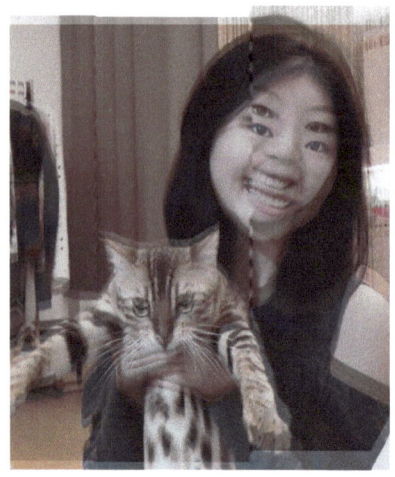

JIA ZHONG, Judge
She graduated from the Illustration Department at the School of Visual Arts in New York. Her work explores the intricate relationship between humanity and nature through a series of imaginative landscape paintings. By highlighting the profound necessity for reverence toward nature, her art captures its spirit—celebrating both its beauty and formidable power. Echoing Shakespeare's sentiment that "All the world's a stage," she employs her art to unveil the natural world's grandeur, turning every canvas into a stage where nature's majesty plays the lead role.

YAXIN TU, Judge

She holds a degree from the Illustration Department at the School of Visual Arts in New York and is currently pursuing a degree in Art Business at Sotheby's Institute of Art. With a robust foundation in painting and an early immersion in the art scene, she has developed a rich understanding of the art world's various facets, enhanced by a global perspective. Her expertise spans printmaking, watercolor, and oil painting. Presently, she is delving into the realm of digital art and aspires to establish herself as a digital artist through forthcoming exhibitions.

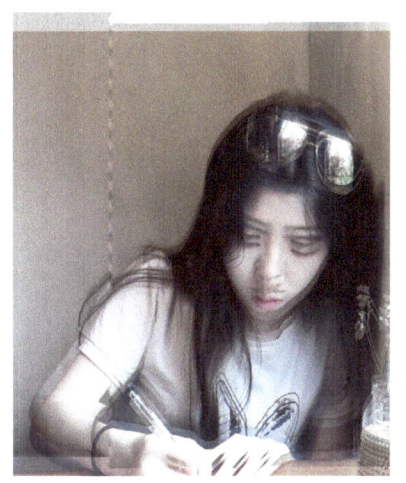

EMIRI FUJIMOTO, Judge

Emiri's practice revolves around performative action, sculpture, and installation. Born in Japan and raised in China, her work delves into themes of displacement and transience with the sweetest wishes of "everything will be okay <3". She earned her a BFA from the School of Visual Arts and now pursuing an MFA Sculpture from Cranbrook Academy of Art.

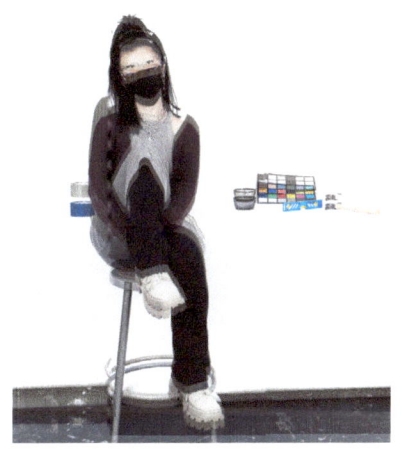

FANGNI WU, Judge

She graduated from the Illustration Department at the School of Visual Arts in New York, where she honed a distinctive style characterized by vibrant colors, intricate patterns, and meticulous attention to detail. In 2020, she showcased and sold her original illustrations at the Shanghai Childrens Book Fair, gaining notable recognition. The following year, she enriched her artistic perspective and experience through volunteer work at Chengdu Luhu A4 Art Museum and Tianfu Art Park. Currently based in Tokyo, Fangni continues to refine her illustration skills, constantly evolving as an artist.

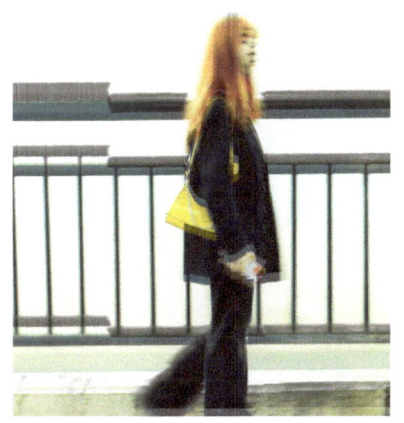

Contents

Elaine V. Kuang 2
Jiajun Deng 10
Ziyan Chen 18
Rong Hong 28
Lujia Gao 36
Yuiyan Wan 44
Xiyu Zhang 50
Yihan Hu 56
Emma Chen 62
The "Vibrant Future" International Education Project for Young Artists Publications List..................................68
The Young Picture Book Artists Program Publications List..69
Publication Information..70

VIBRANT VISIONS
International Youth Artist Artwork Series-5

ELAINE V. KUANG
ArtCenter College of Design, USA

- Gold Award for Art, 6th Liberty Awards, International Society of Young Artists, USA, 2023.
- Person of the Year 2022, International Society of Young Artists, USA, 2022.
- Gold Award for Art, 5th Liberty Awards, International Society of Young Artists, USA, 2022.
- Person of the Year 2021, International Society of Young Artists, USA, 2021.
- Gold Award for Art, 4th Liberty Awards, International Society of Young Artists, USA, 2021.
- Gold Award for Art, 3rd Liberty Awards, International Society of Young Artists, USA, 2020.
- Person of the Year 2019, International Society of Young Artists, USA, 2019.
- Gold Award for Art, 2nd Liberty Awards, International Society of Young Artists, USA, 2019.
- Bronze Award for Art, 1st Liberty Awards, International Society of Young Artists, USA, 2018.

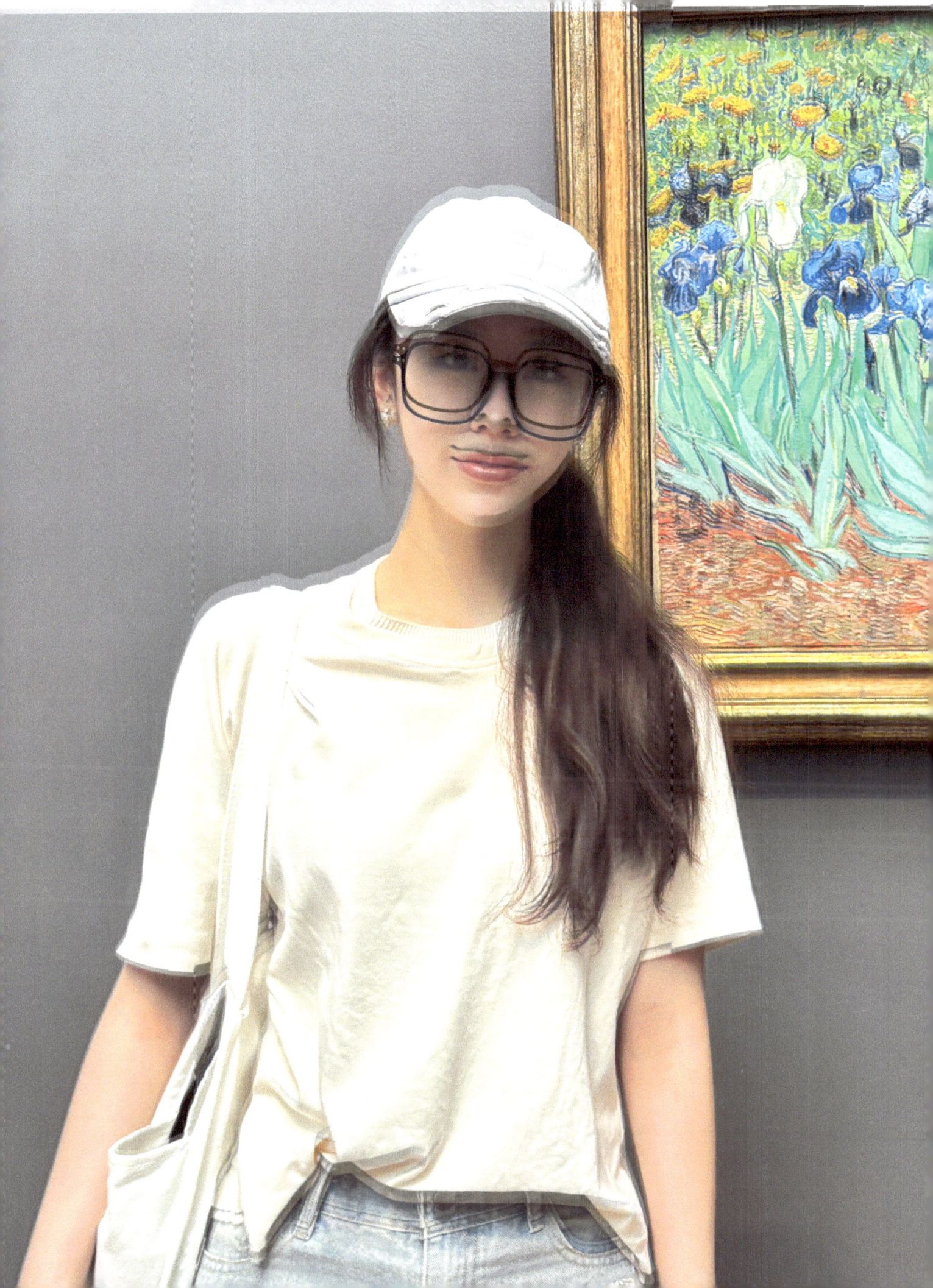

International Youth Artist Artwork Series-5

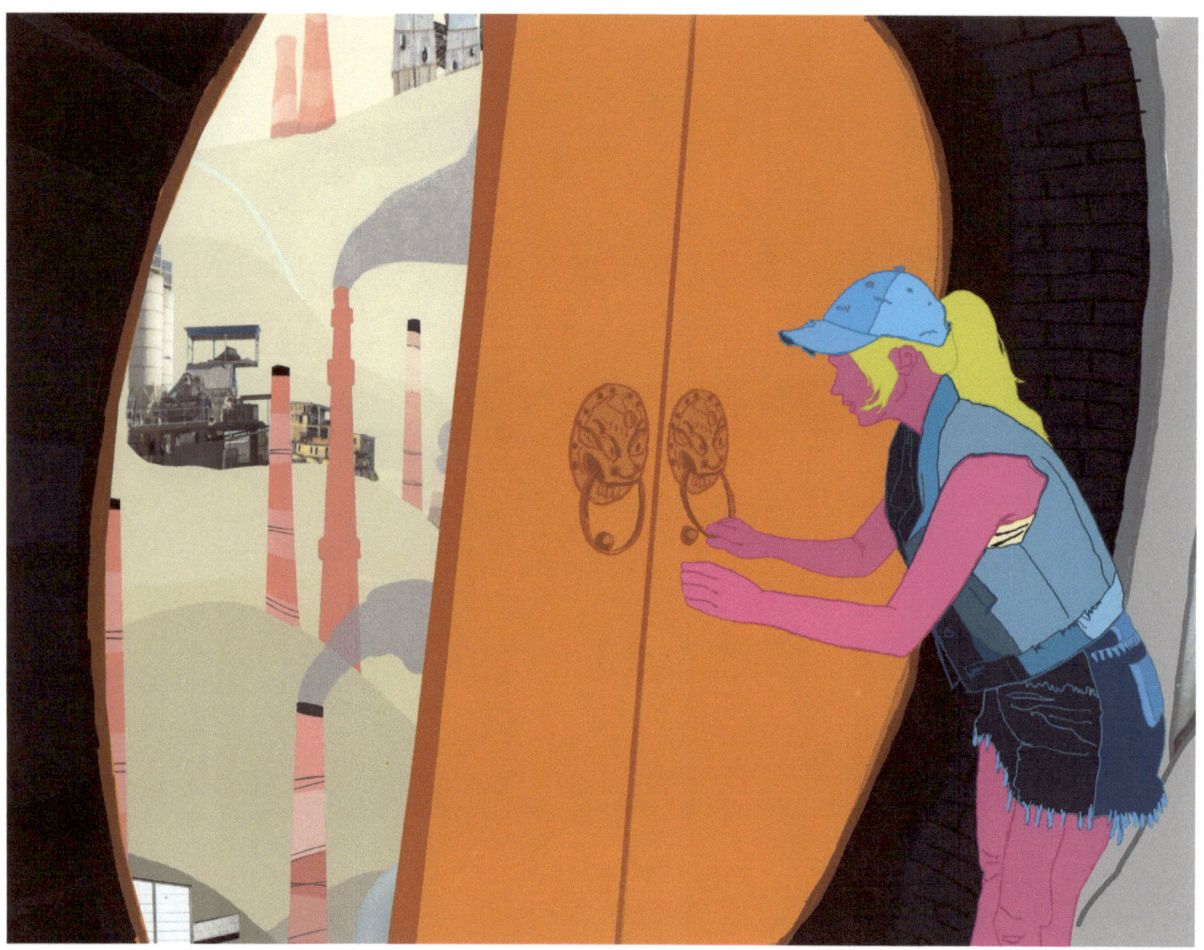

Door, digital

Vibrant Visions

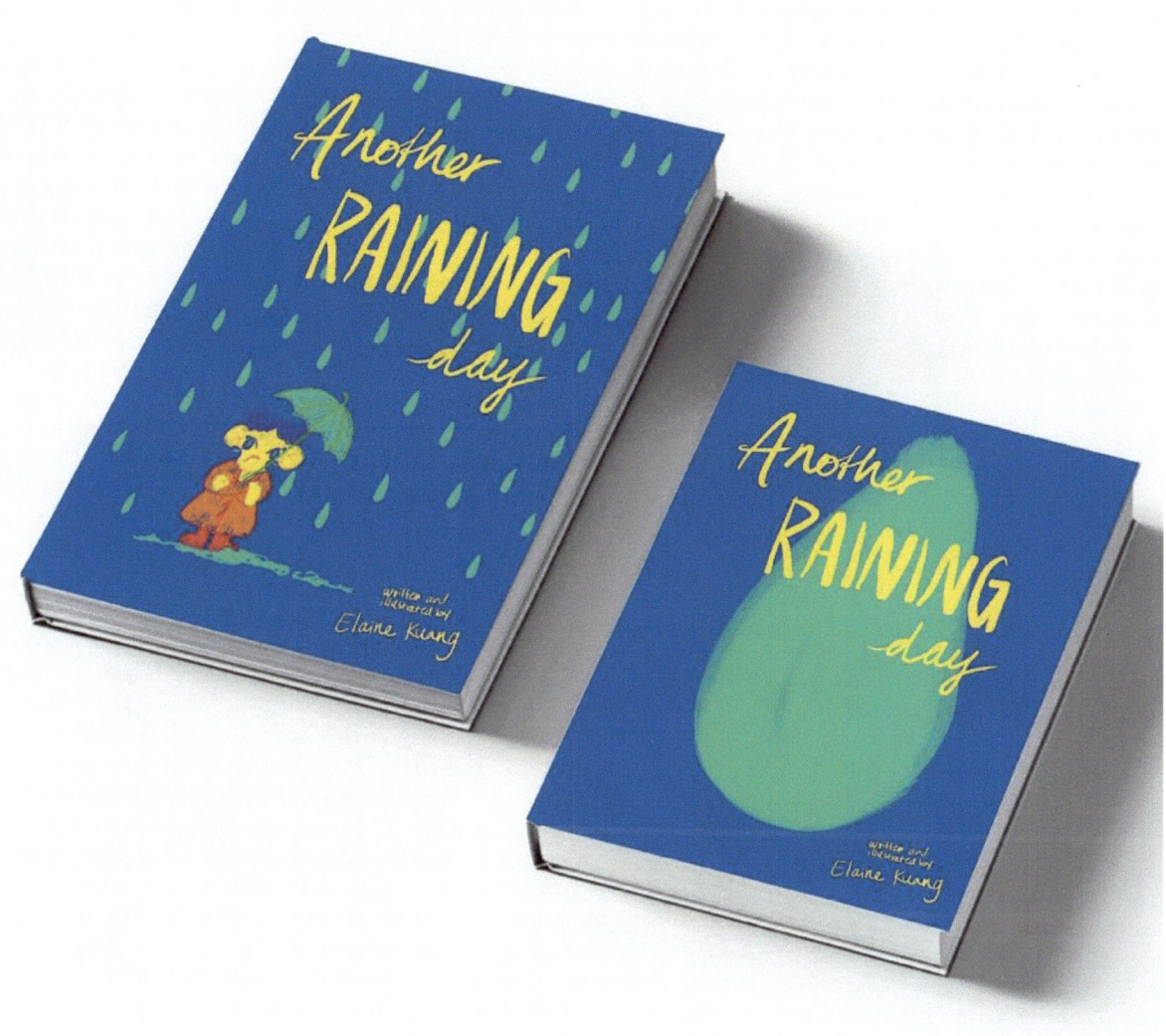

Another Raining Day, digital book mockup

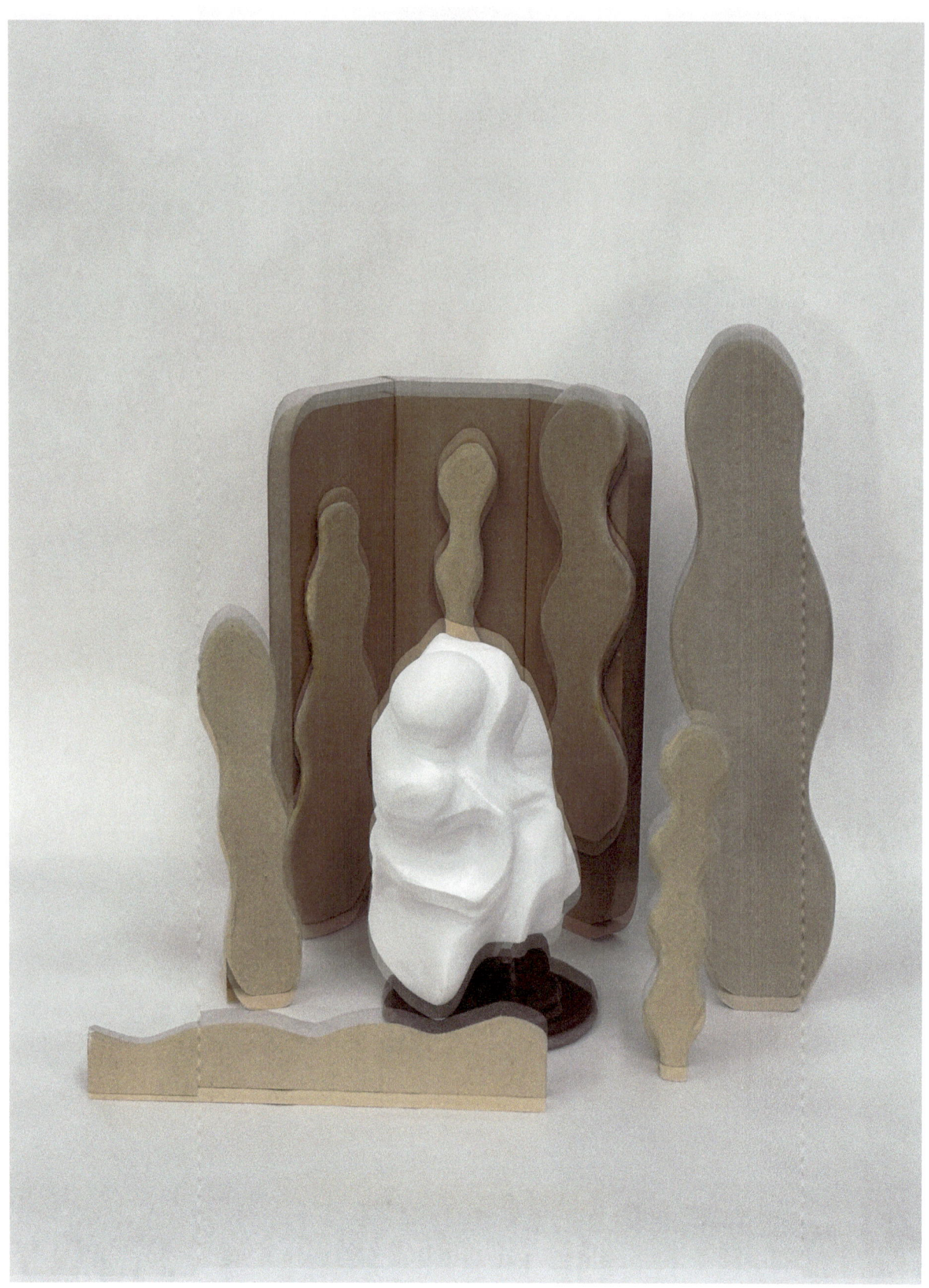

Willow, Plaster sculpture with wood

Vibrant Visions

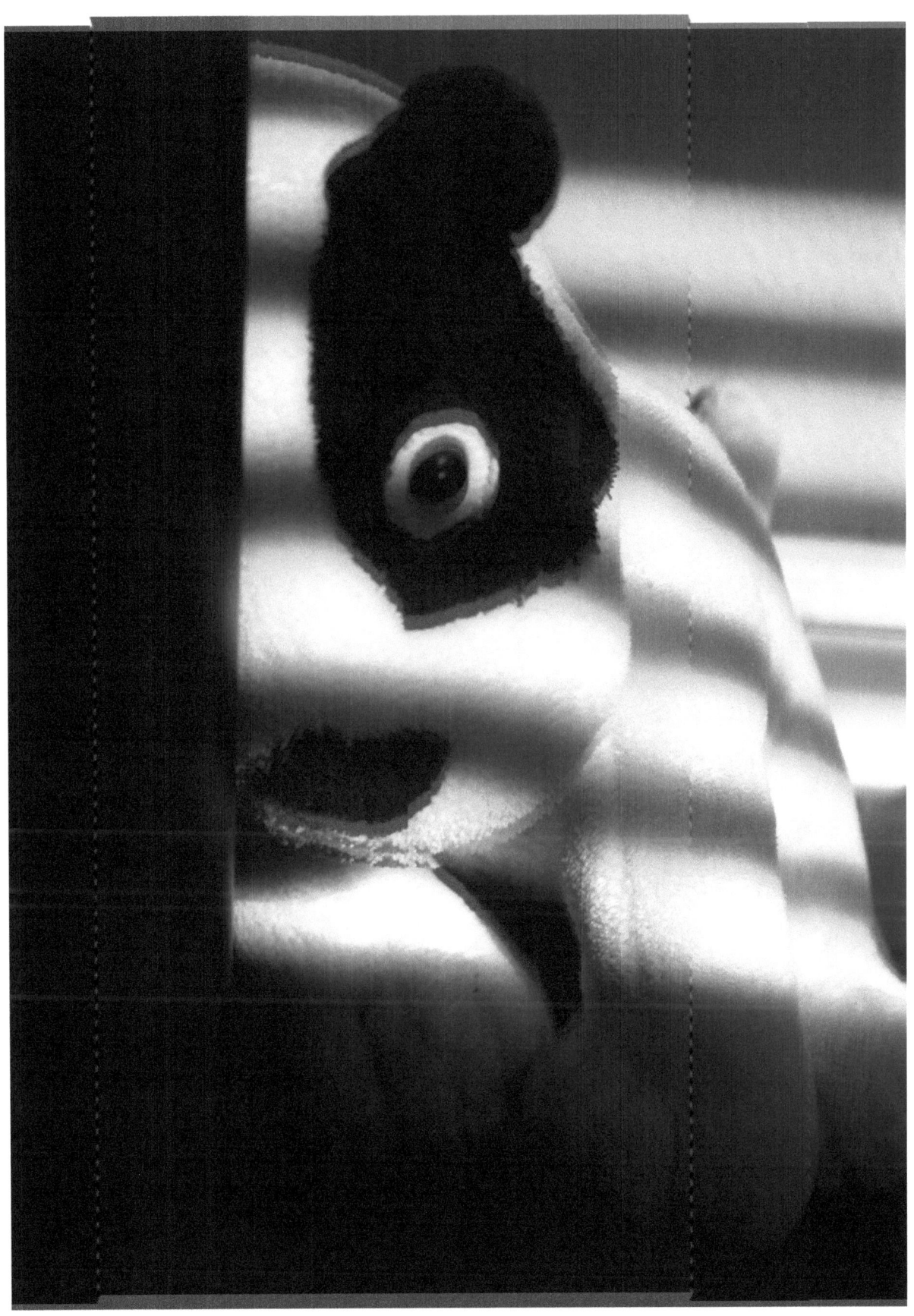

The Silent Observer, photography

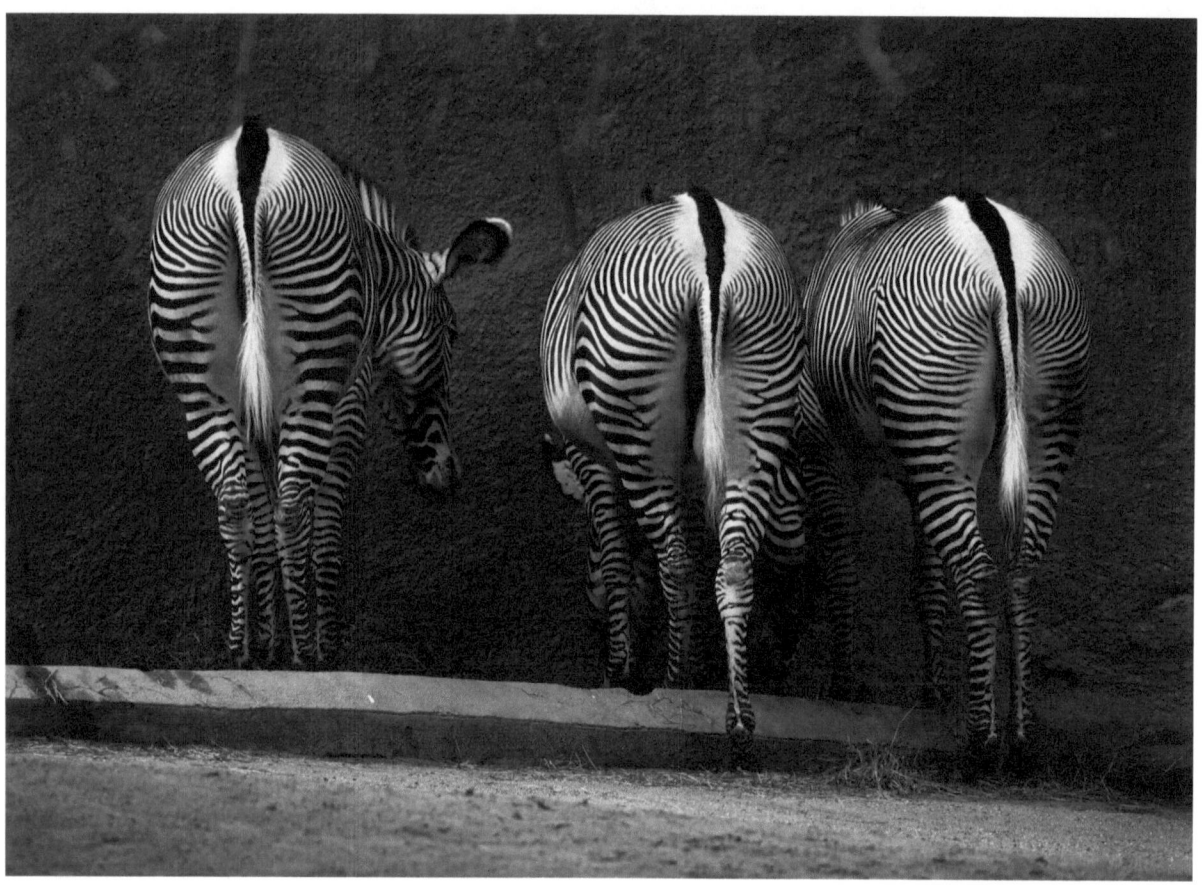

Murmur, photography

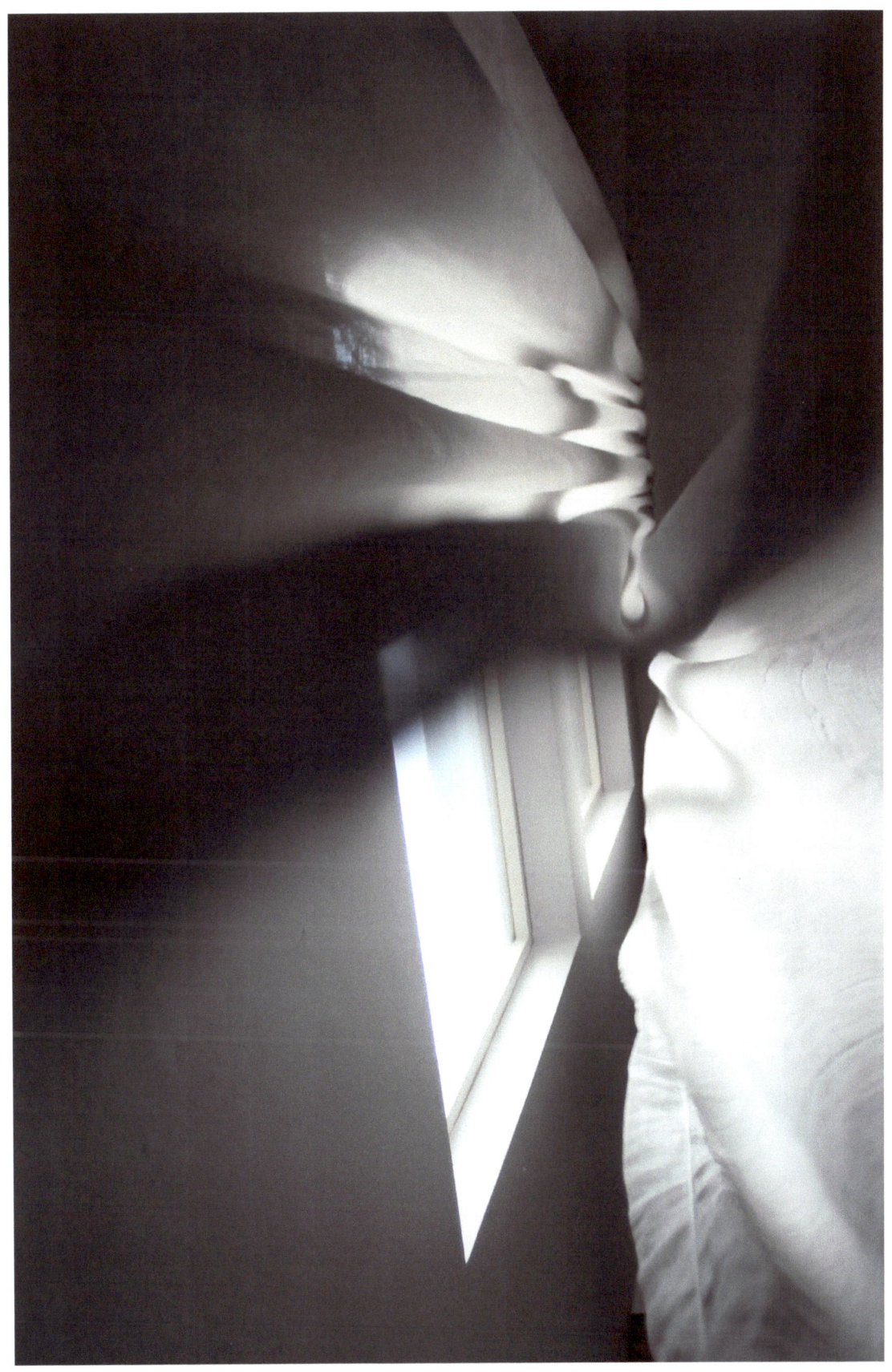

The Ephemeral Dance, Photography

JIAJUN DENG
California College of the Arts, USA

- Gold Award for Art, 6th Liberty Awards, International Society of Young Artists, USA, 2023.
- Gold Award for Art, 5th Liberty Awards, International Society of Young Artists, USA, 2022.
- Gold Award for Art, 4th Liberty Awards, International Society of Young Artists, USA, 2021.
- Person of the Year 2020, International Society of Young Artists, USA, 2020.
- Gold Award for Art, 3rd Liberty Awards, International Society of Young Artists, USA, 2020.
- Silver Award for Art, 2nd Liberty Awards, International Society of Young Artists, USA, 2019.
- Gold Award for Art, 1st Liberty Awards, International Society of Young Artists, USA, 2018.
- Gold Award, "The Colorful Peace" Art Project Honoring the 100th Anniversary of the WWI Armistice, International Society of Young Artists, USA, 2018.

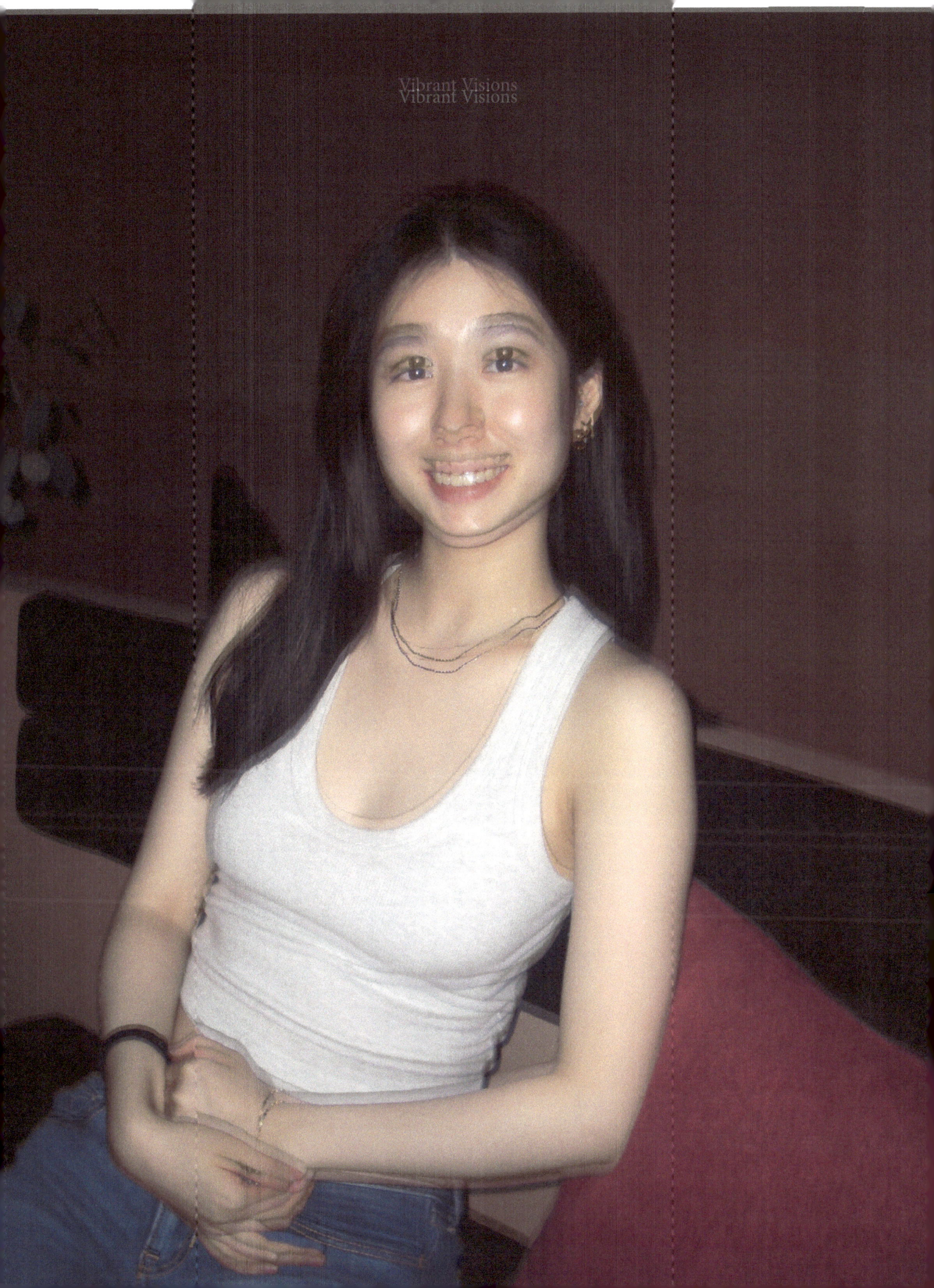

International Youth Artist Artwork Series-5

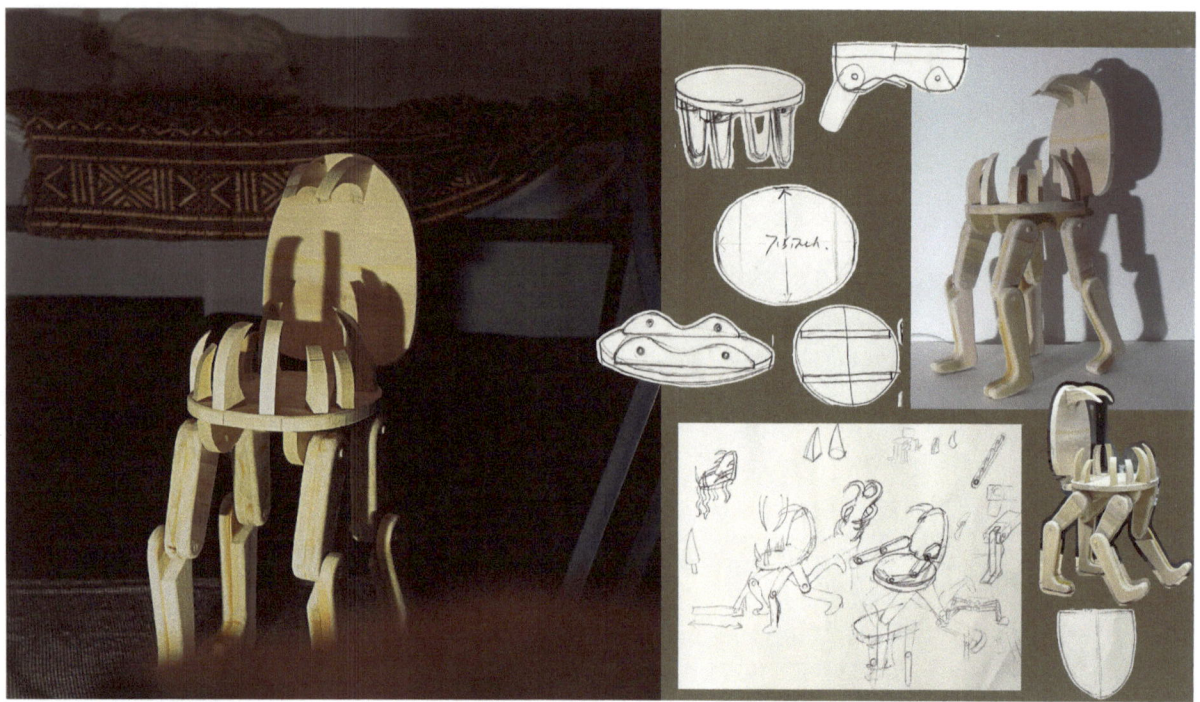

Running Chair, wood

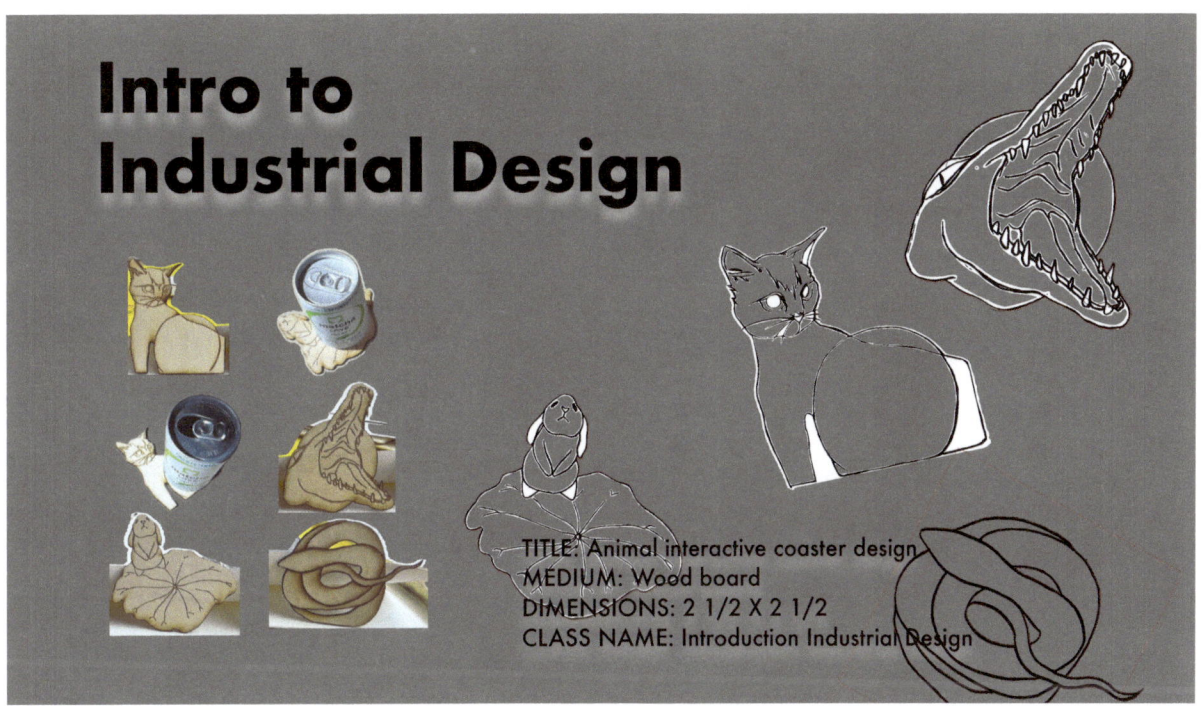

Animal Interactive Coaster Design, wood board

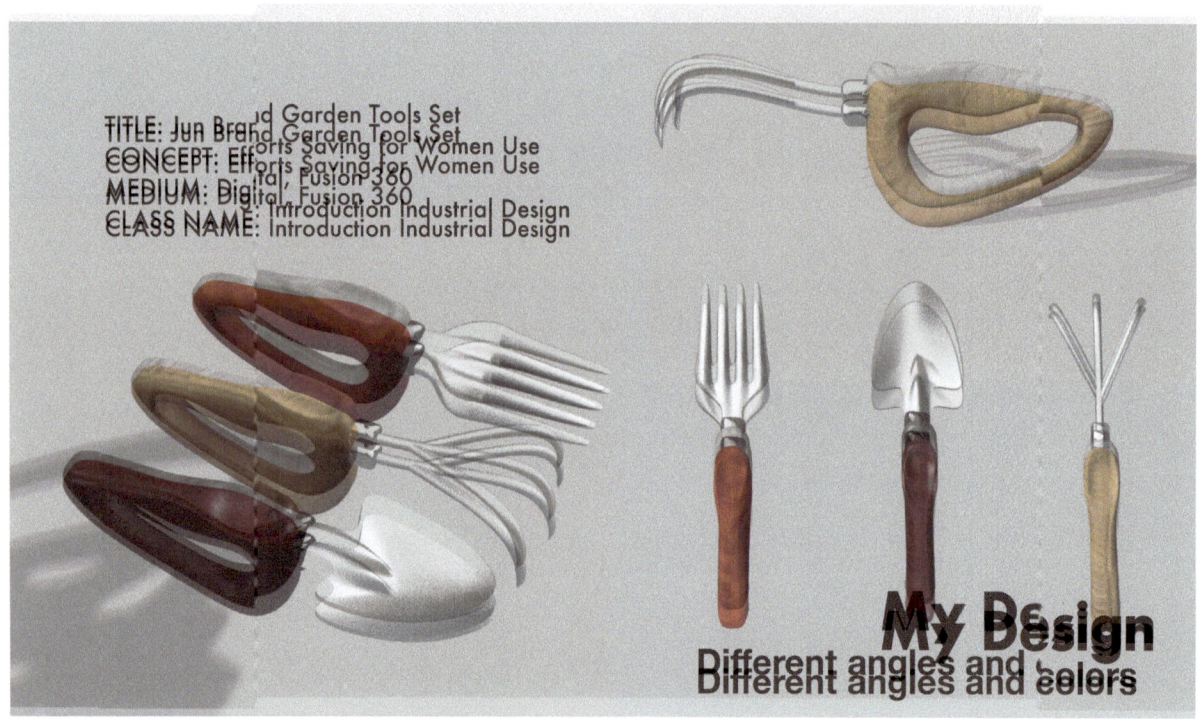

Jun Brand Garden Tools Set, digital

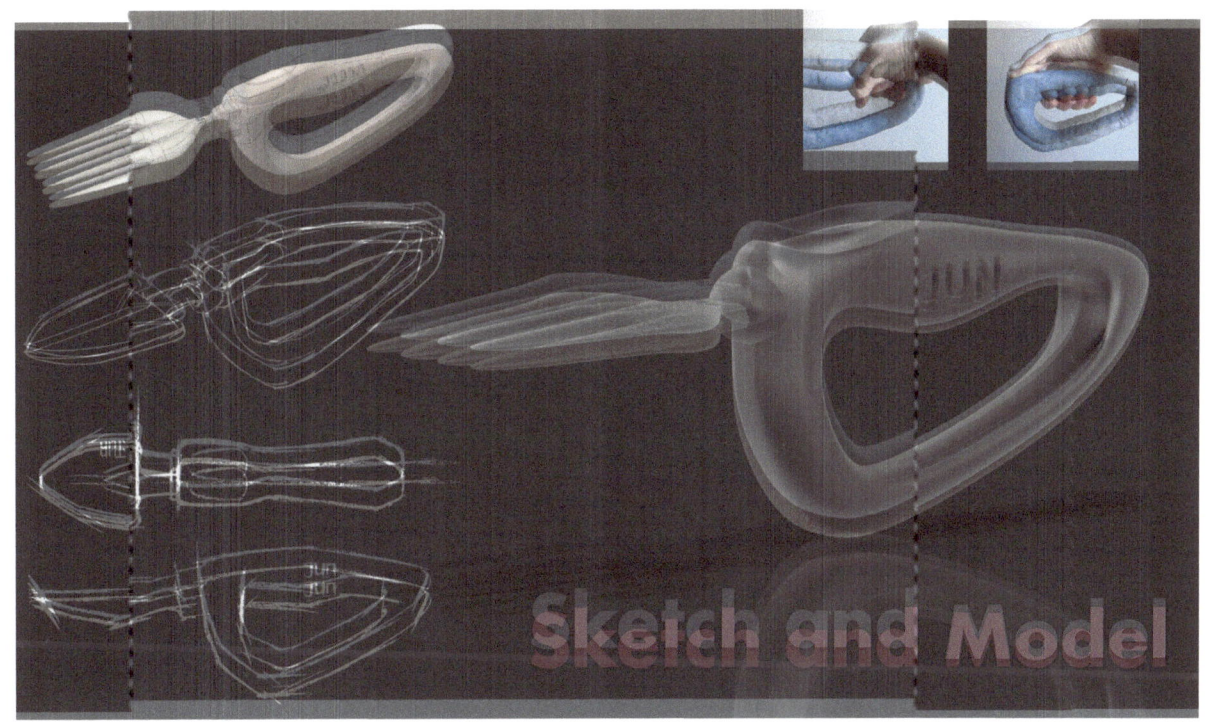

Sketch and Model, digital

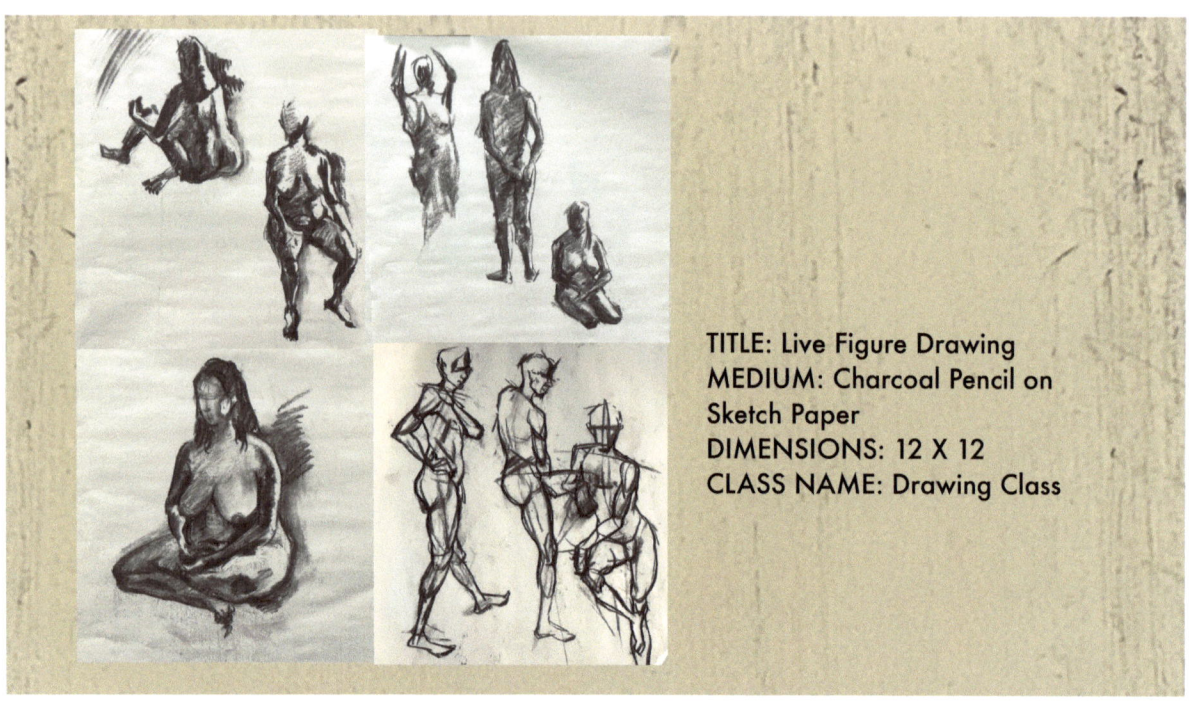

Live Figure Drawing, pencil on paper

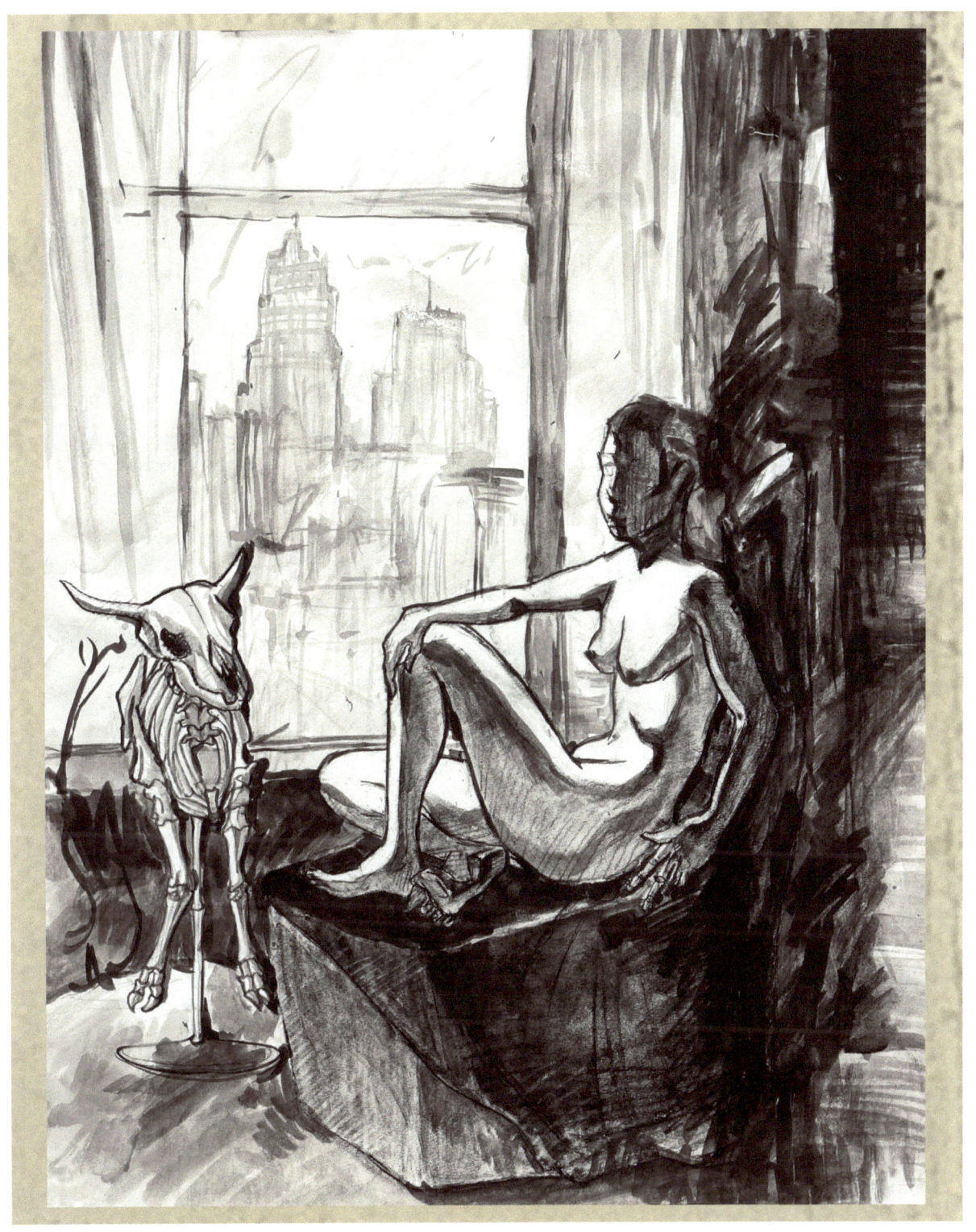

Live Figure Drawing, pencil on paper

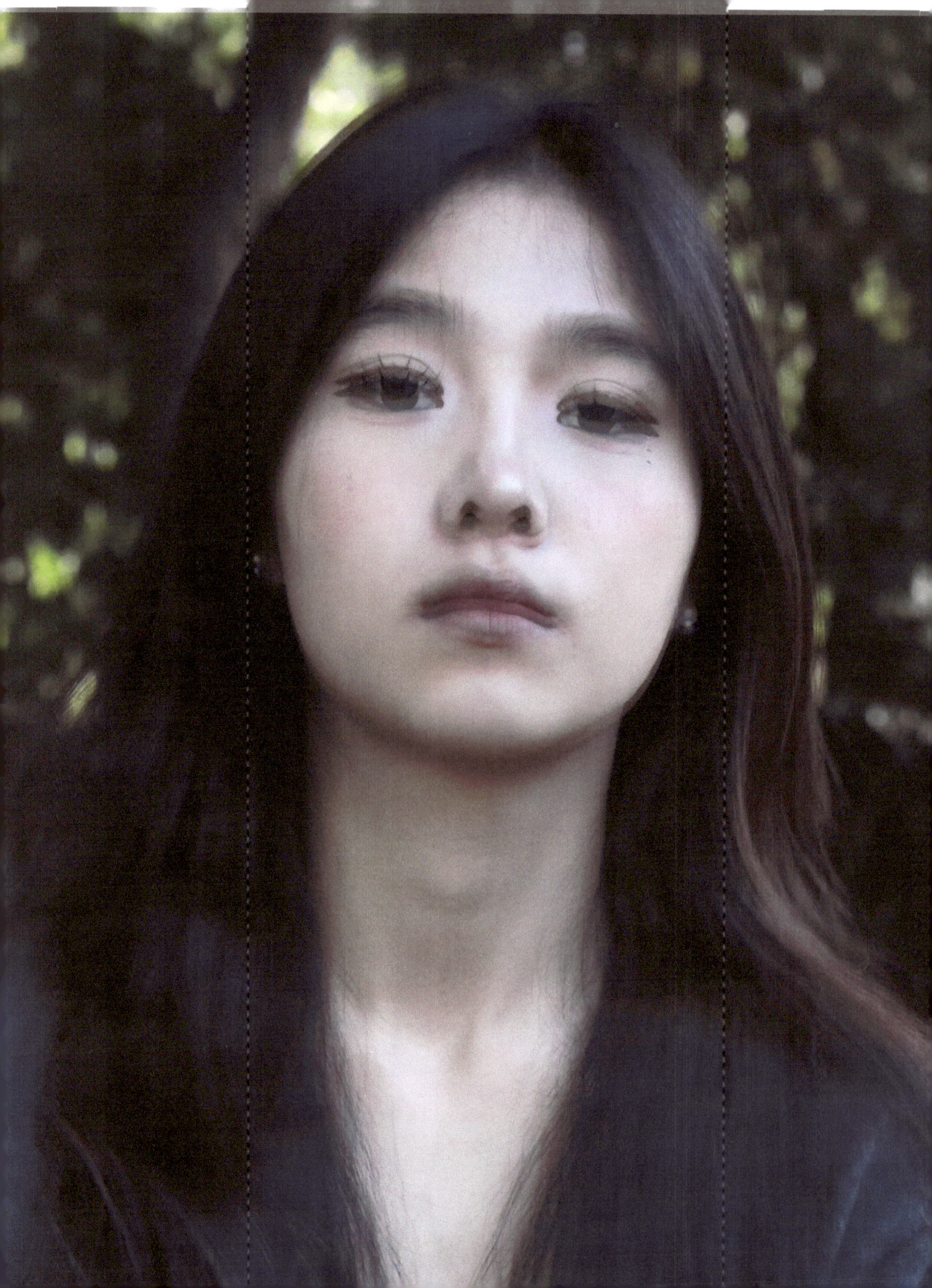

Ziyan Chen, a dedicated member of the International Society of Young Artists (ISOYA), has been named the "Person of the Year 2023." Throughout the year, Ziyan demonstrated remarkable commitment to mastering the art of painting, tirelessly overcoming numerous challenges encountered along the learning journey. Her diligence in practice and thoughtful understanding of artistic concepts led to significant breakthroughs in her studies. Ziyan's perseverance and the impressive progress she made in her artistic endeavors are what distinguished her this year, earning her this well-deserved recognition from ISOYA.

Ziyan Chen

PERSON OF THE YEAR 2023

ZIYAN CHEN
Ruben S. Ayala High School, USA

- **Person of the Year 2023, International Society of Young Artists, USA, 2023.**
- **Silver Award for Art, 6th Liberty Awards, International Society of Young Artists, USA, 2023.**
- **Silver Award for Art, 5th Liberty Awards, International Society of Young Artists, USA, 2022.**
- **Gold Award for Art, 4th Liberty Awards, International Society of Young Artists, USA, 2021.**
- **Gold Award for Art, 3rd Liberty Awards, International Society of Young Artists, USA, 2020.**
- **Gold Award for Art, 2nd Liberty Awards, International Society of Young Artists, USA, 2019.**

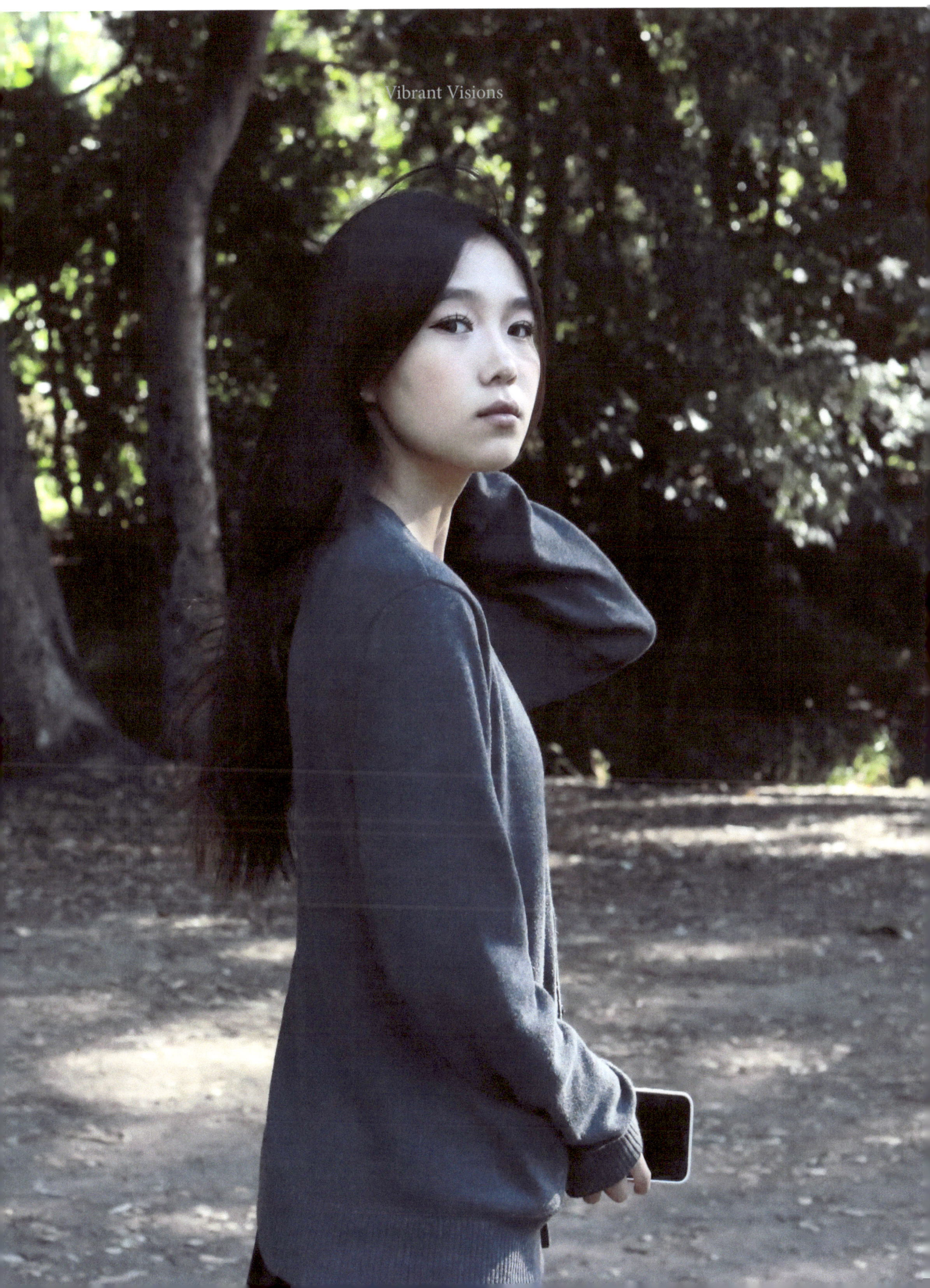

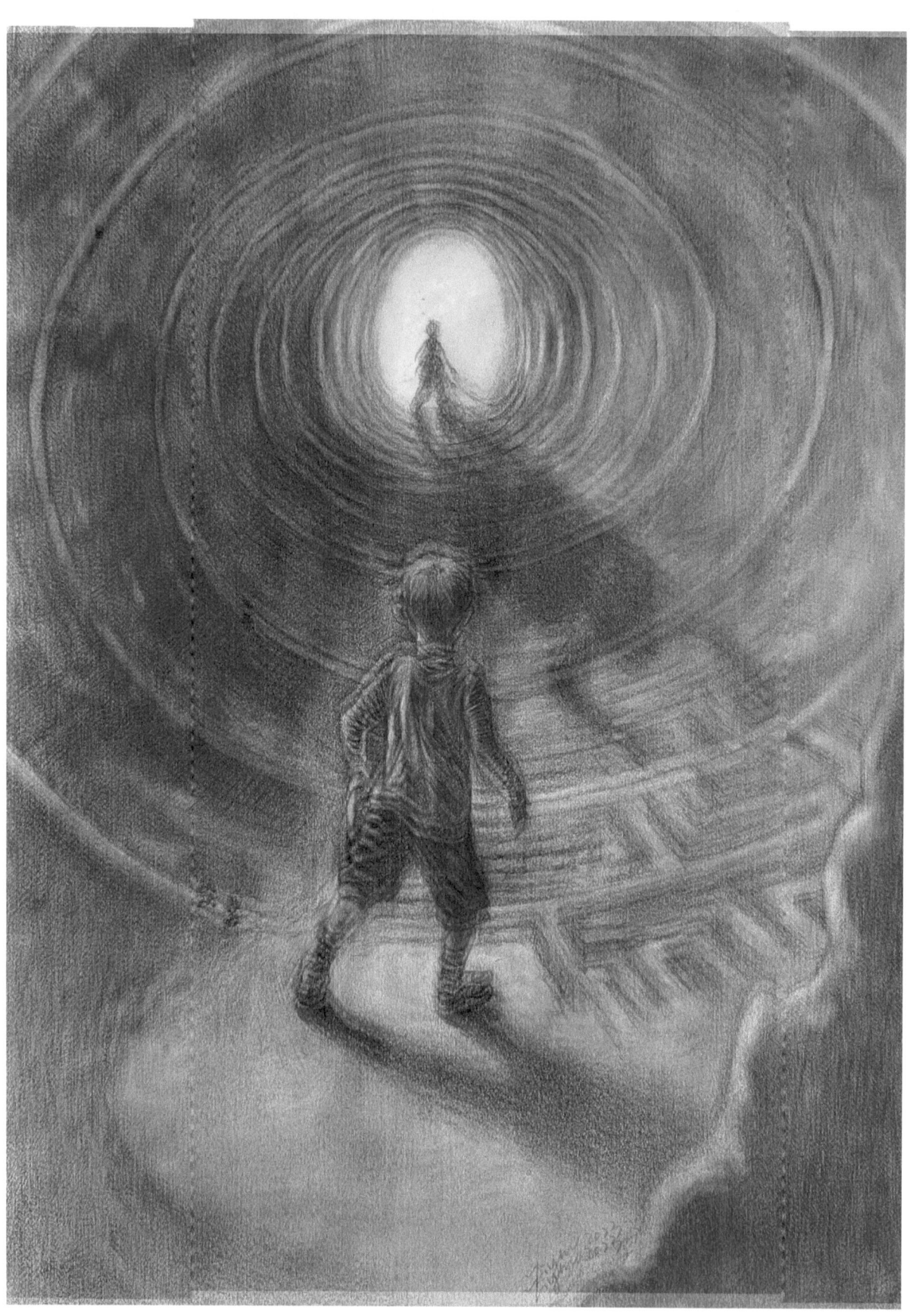

The Maze, pencil on paper

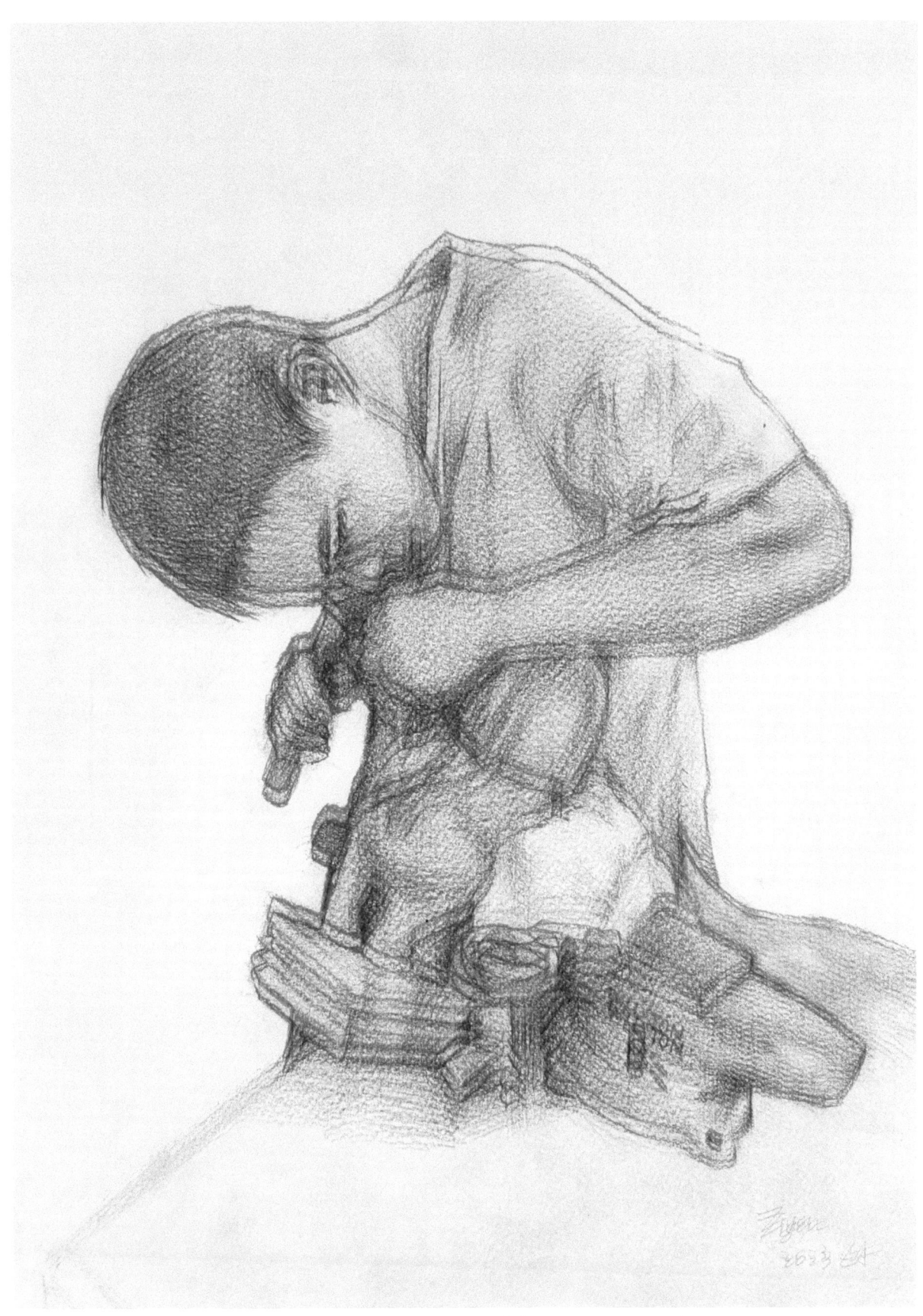

The Young Woodcarver, pencil on paper

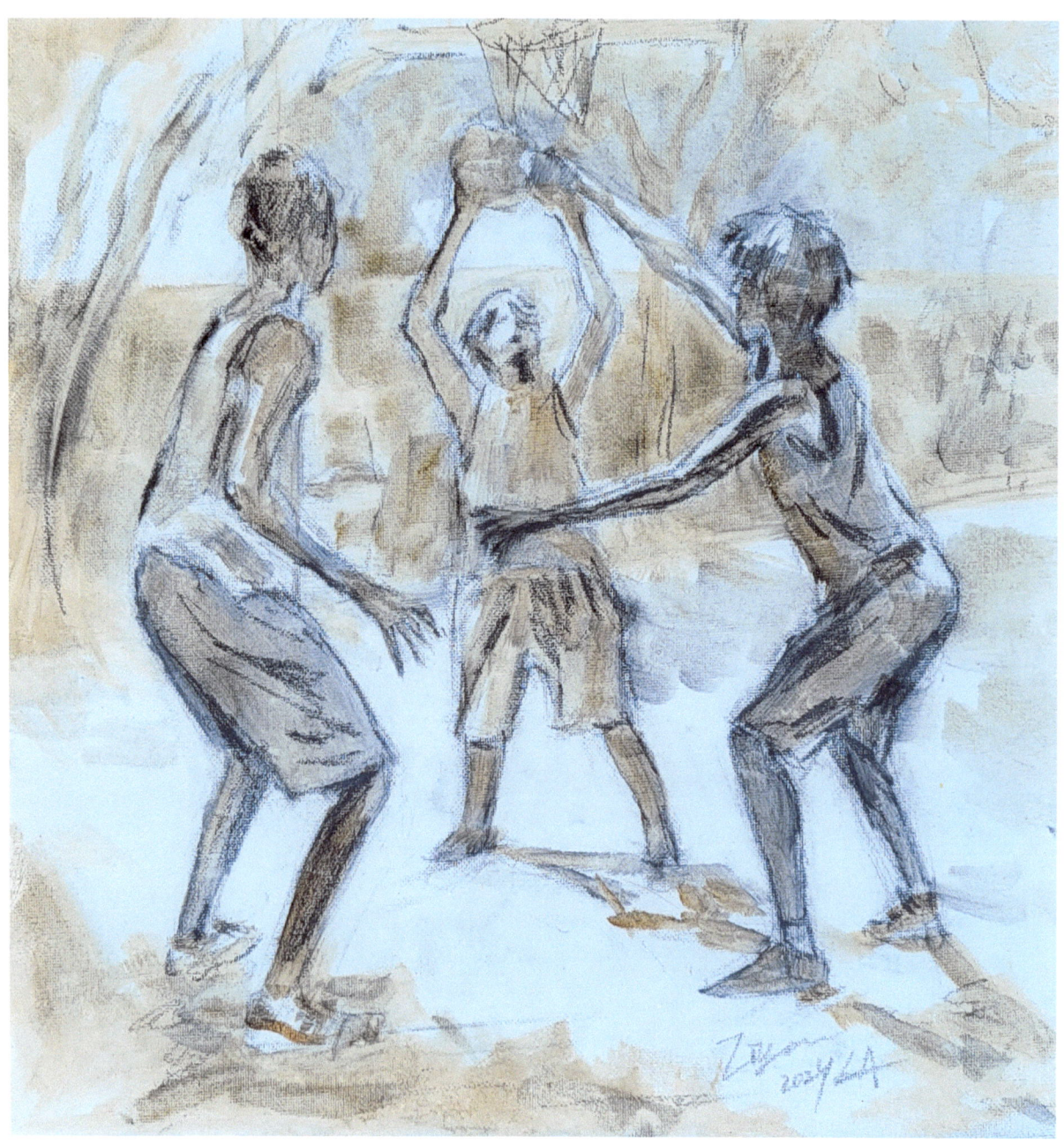

Children Playing Basketball, acrylic on Canvas

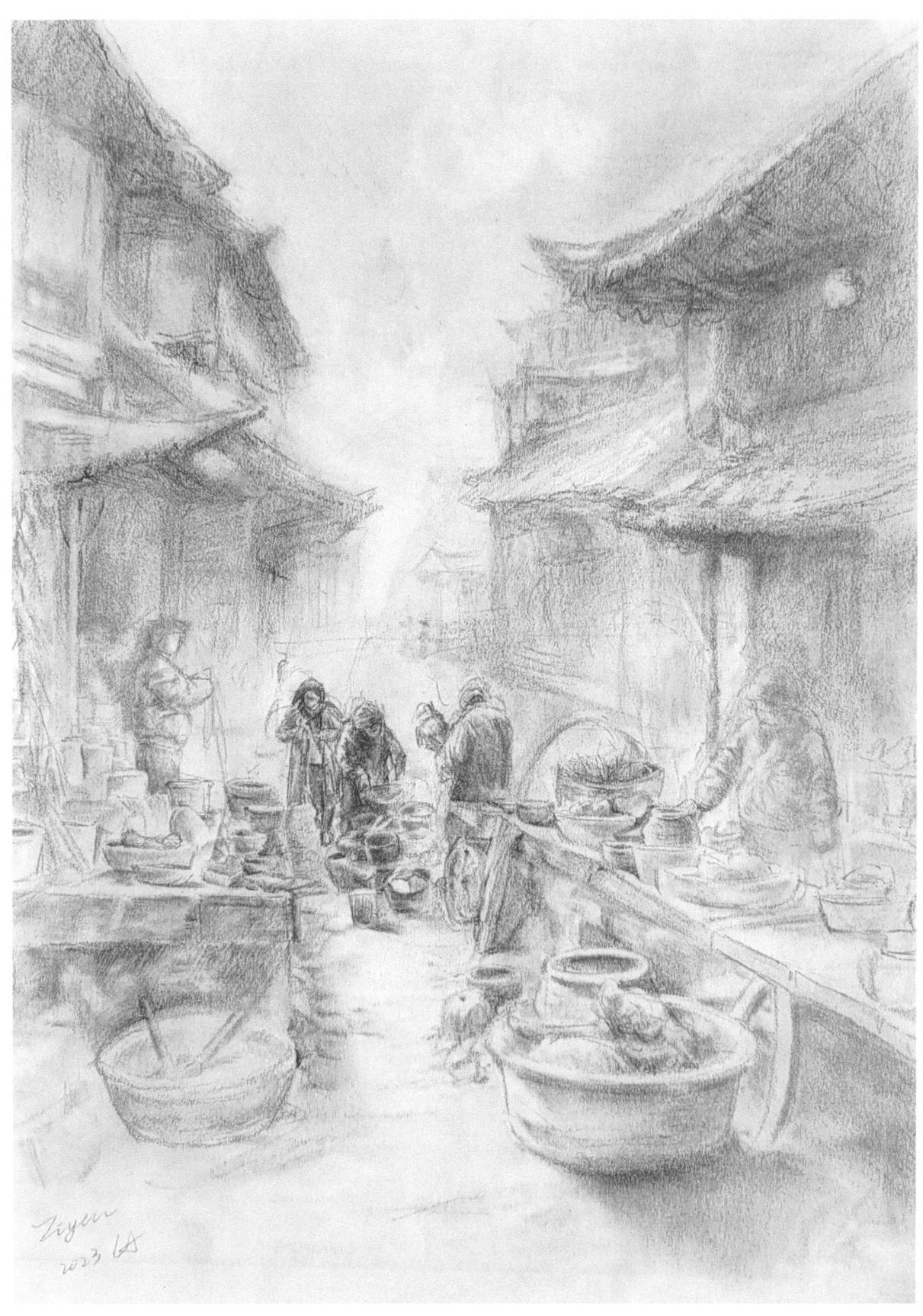

The Old Market, pencil on paper

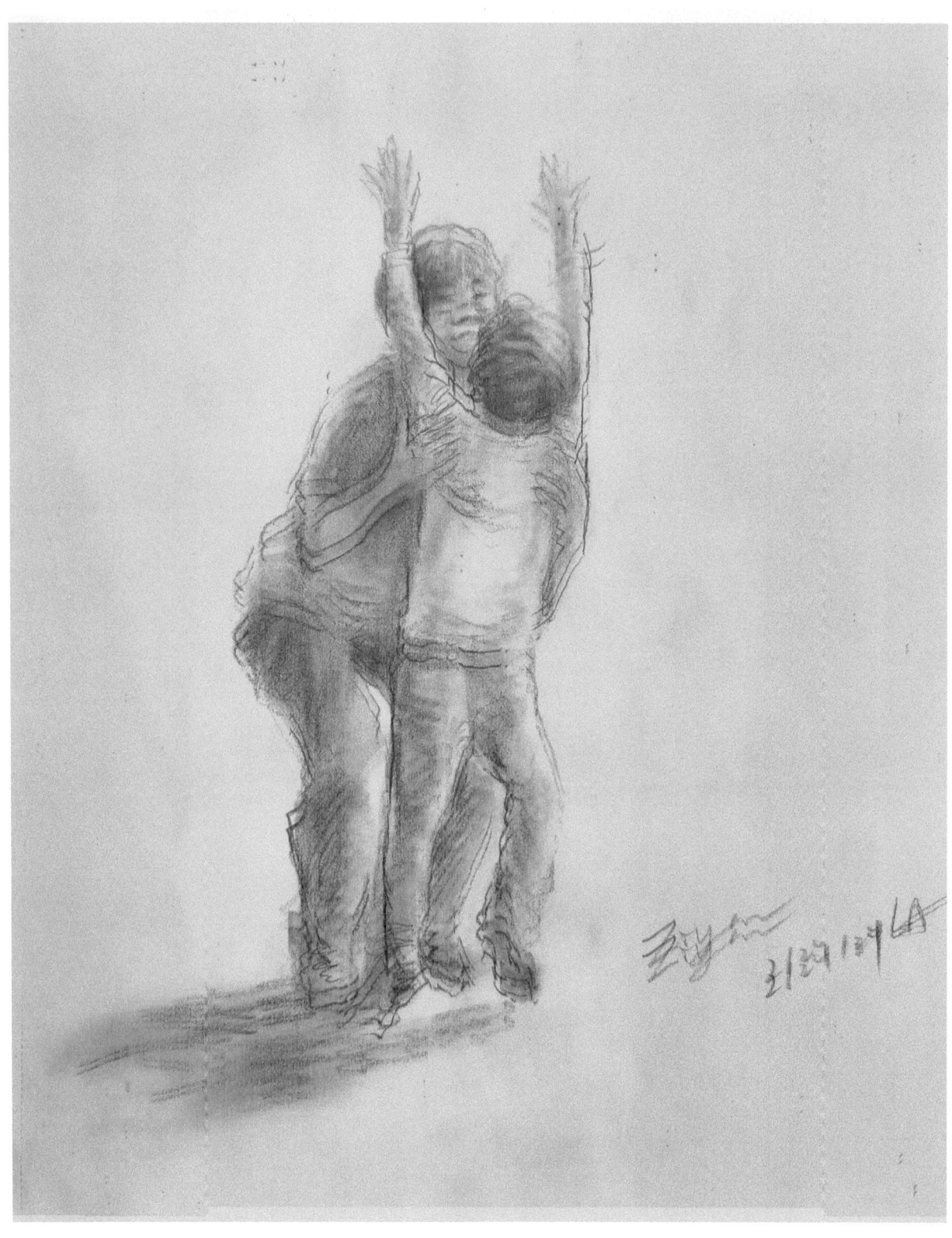

Two Brothers, pencil on paper

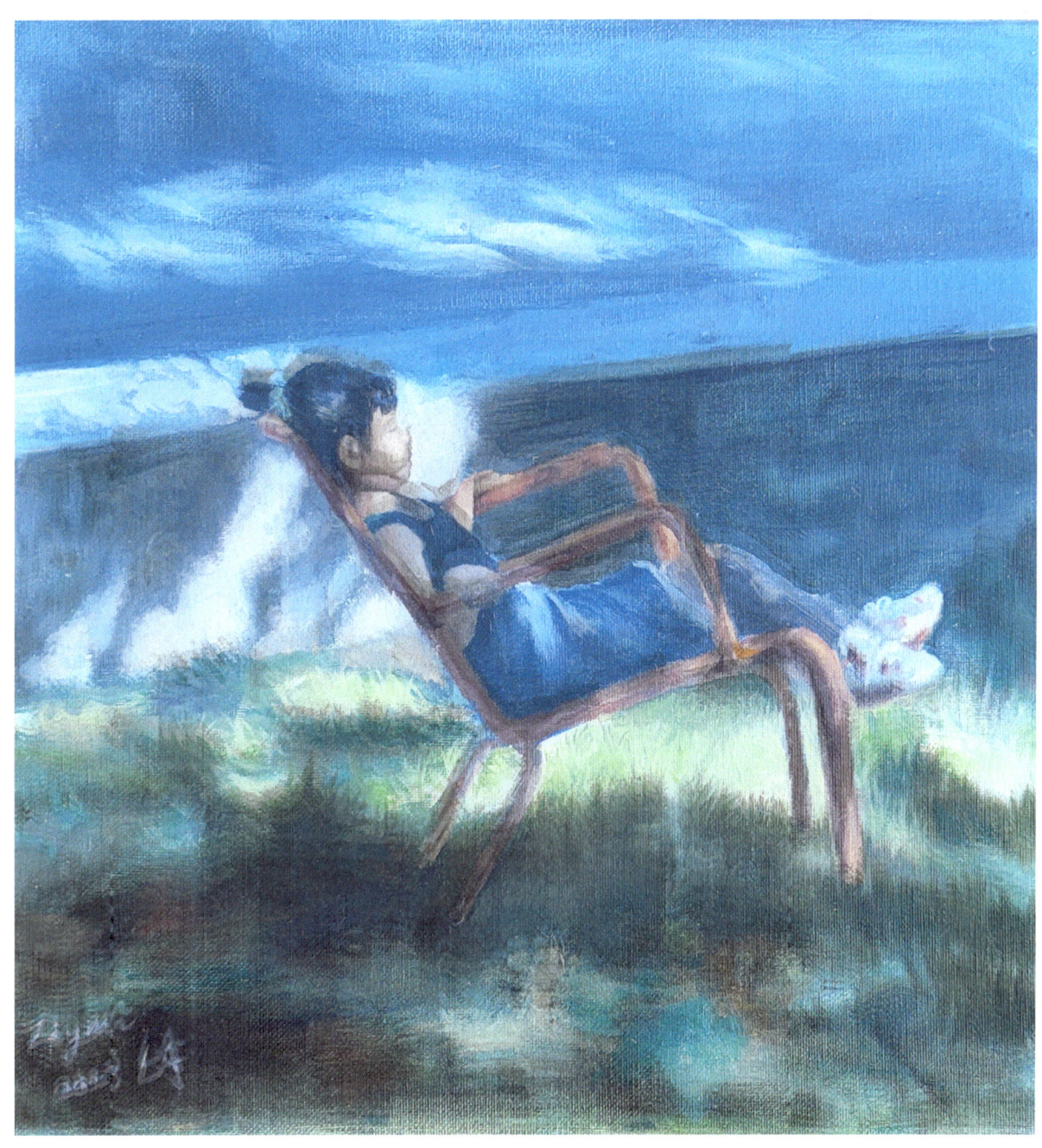

Irence on the Lounge Chair, oil on Canvas

RONG HONG
China University of Geosciences, Wuhan, China

- **Gold Award for Art, 6th Liberty Awards, International Society of Young Artists, USA, 2023.**
- **Gold Award for Art, 2nd Liberty Awards, International Society of Young Artists, 2019.**

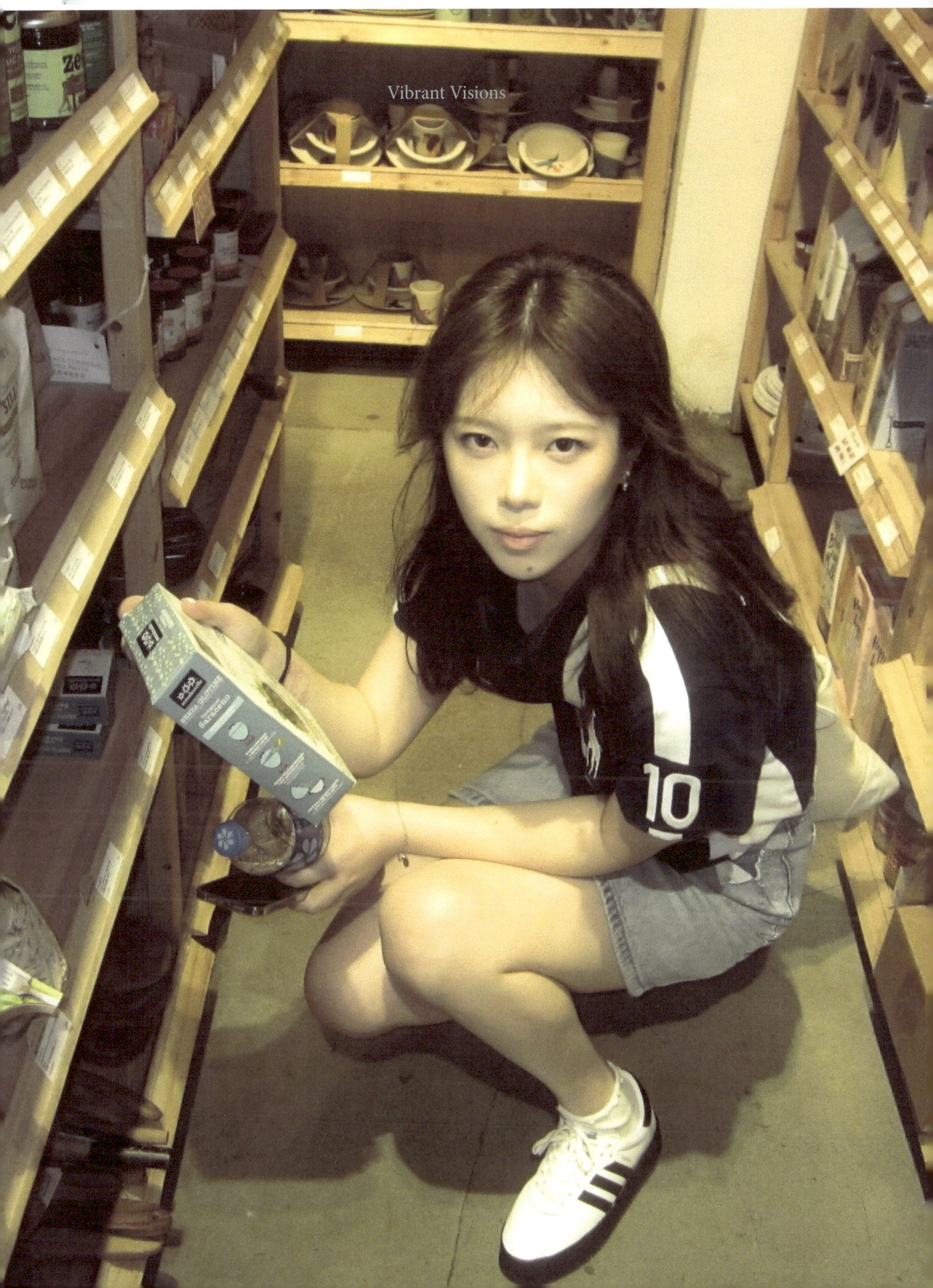

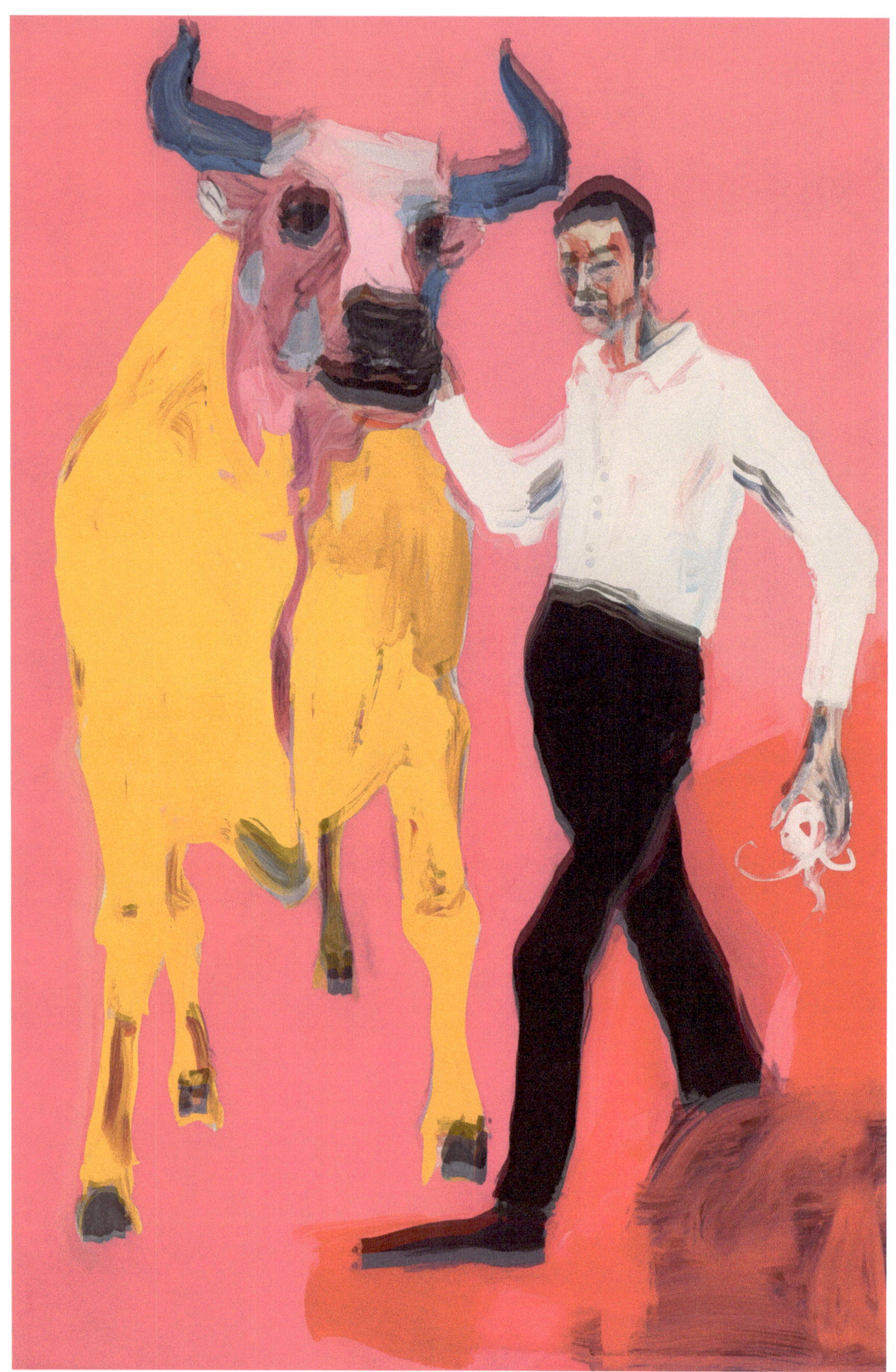

Grant Dancing with the Bull, acrylic on Canvas

Vibrant Visions

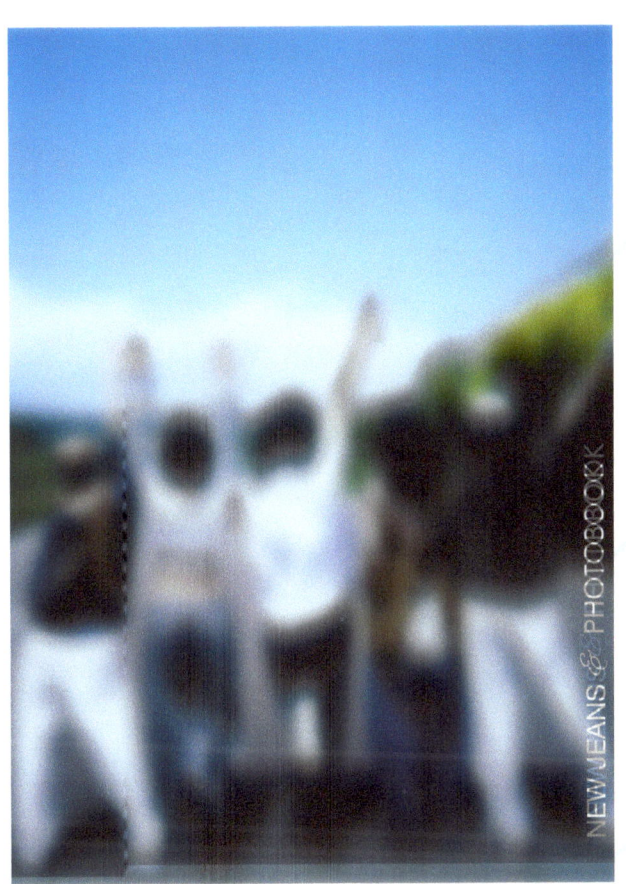
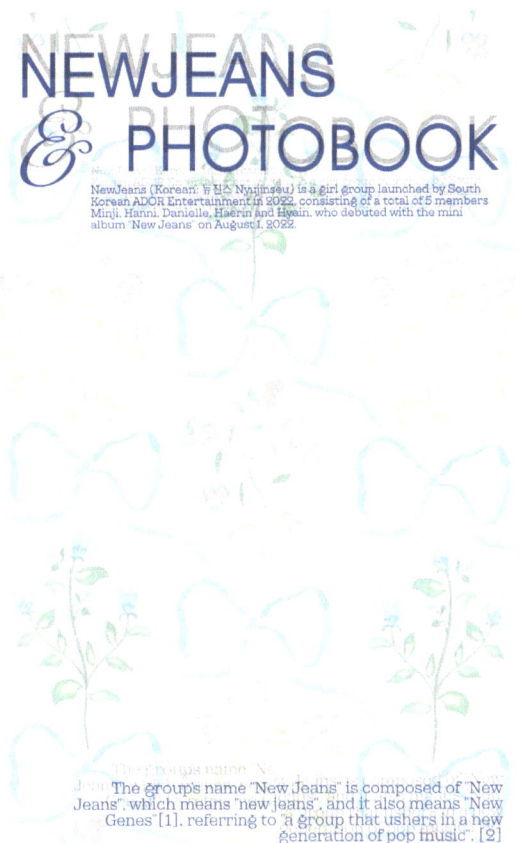

NEWJEANS & PHOTOBOOK

NewJeans (Korean: 뉴진스 Nyujinseu) is a girl group launched by South Korean ADOR Entertainment in 2022, consisting of a total of 5 members Minji, Hanni, Danielle, Haerin and Hyein, who debuted with the mini album "New Jeans" on August 1, 2022.

The group's name "New Jeans" is composed of "New Jeans", which means "new jeans", and it also means "New Genes" [1], referring to "a group that ushers in a new generation of pop music". [2]

Cover and Back Cover of the *Newjeans Photobook*, digital

International Youth Artist Artwork Series-5

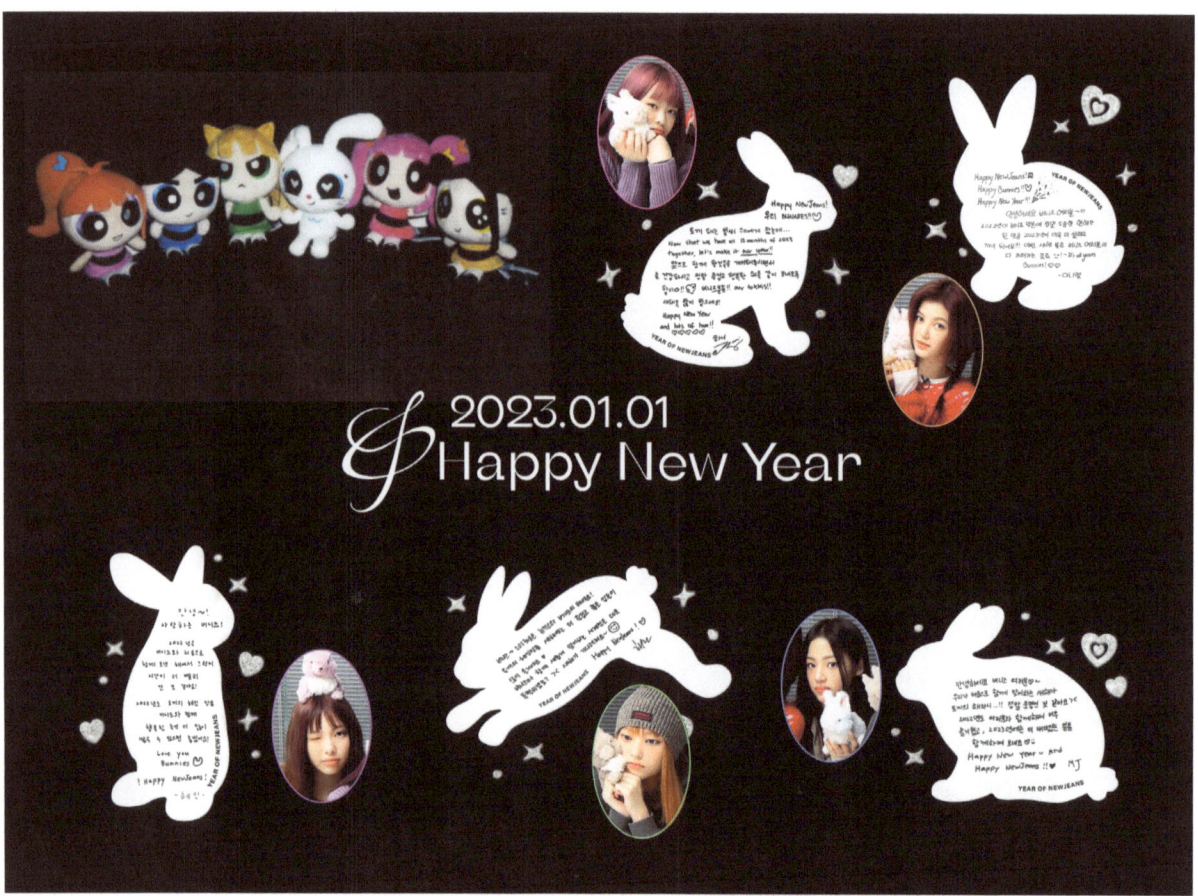

Pages 1 to 2 of the *Newjeans Photobook*, digital

Vibrant Visions

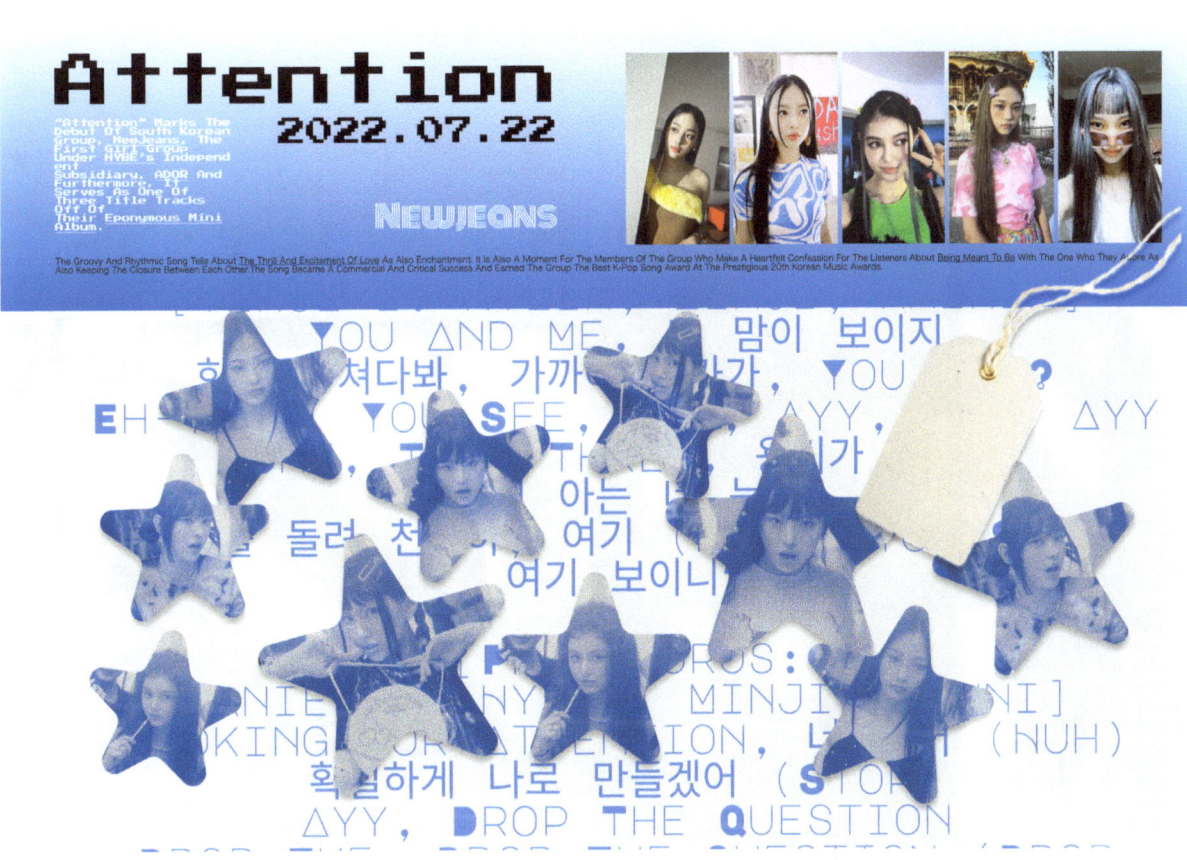

Pages 14 to 15 of the *Newjeans Photobook*, digital

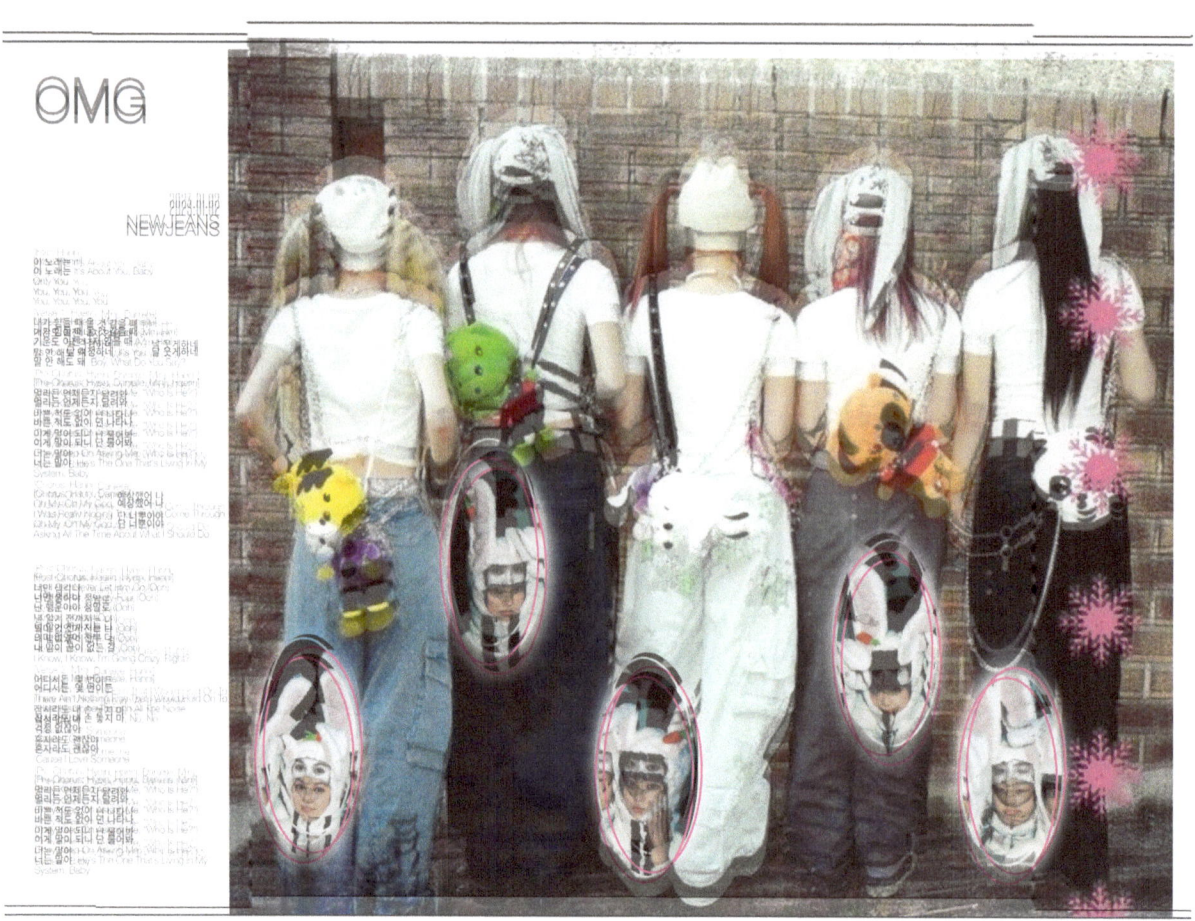

Pages 30 to 31 of the *Newjeans Photobook*, digital

Vibrant Visions

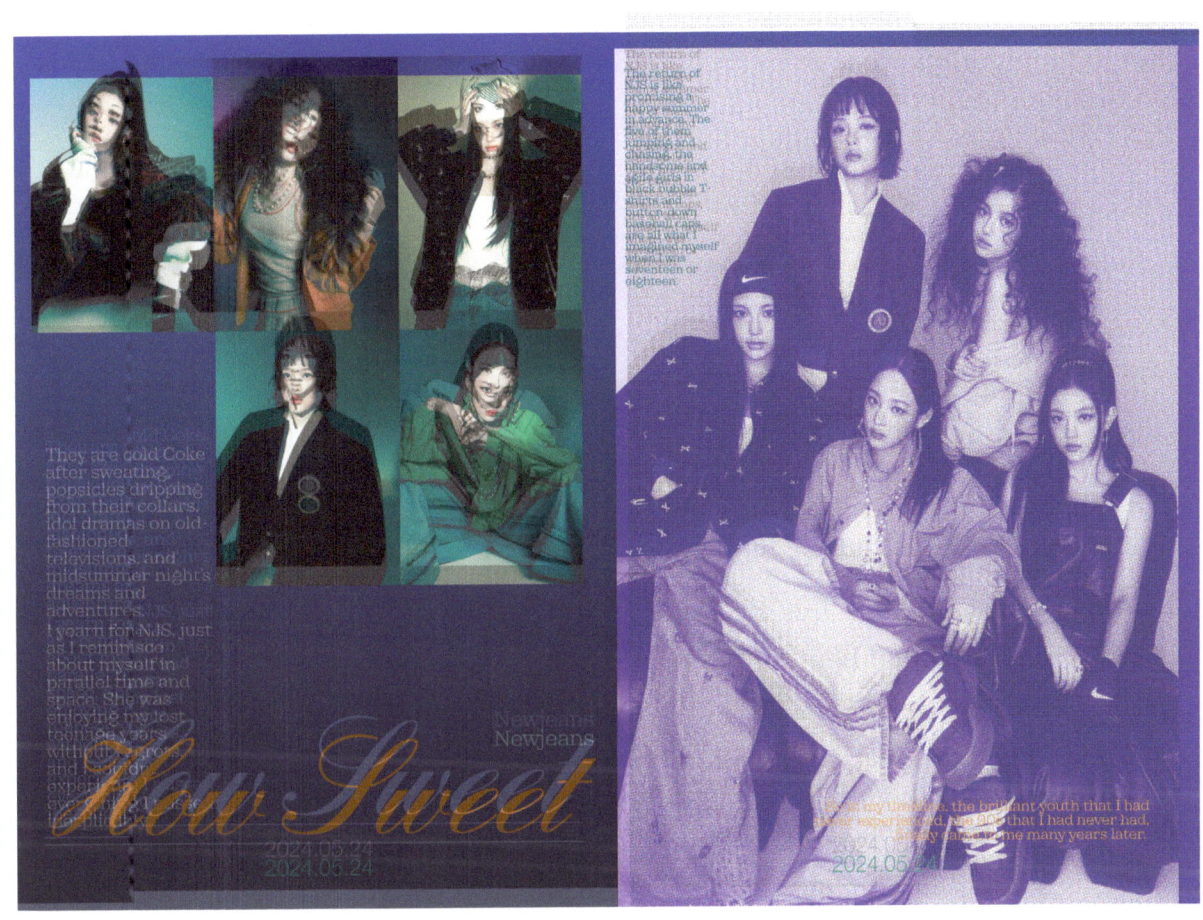

Pages 50 to 51 of the *Newjeans Photobook*, digital

LUJIA GAO
Communication University of Zhejiang, China

- **Silver Award for Art, 6th Liberty Awards, International Society of Young Artists, USA, 2023.**
- **Silver Award for Art, 5th Liberty Awards, International Society of Young Artists, USA, 2022.**
- **2nd Prize, National Creative Composition Competition For Secondary School Students, The writing Academy of China, 2022.**
- **Gold Award for Art, 4th Liberty Awards, International Society of Young Artists, USA, 2021.**

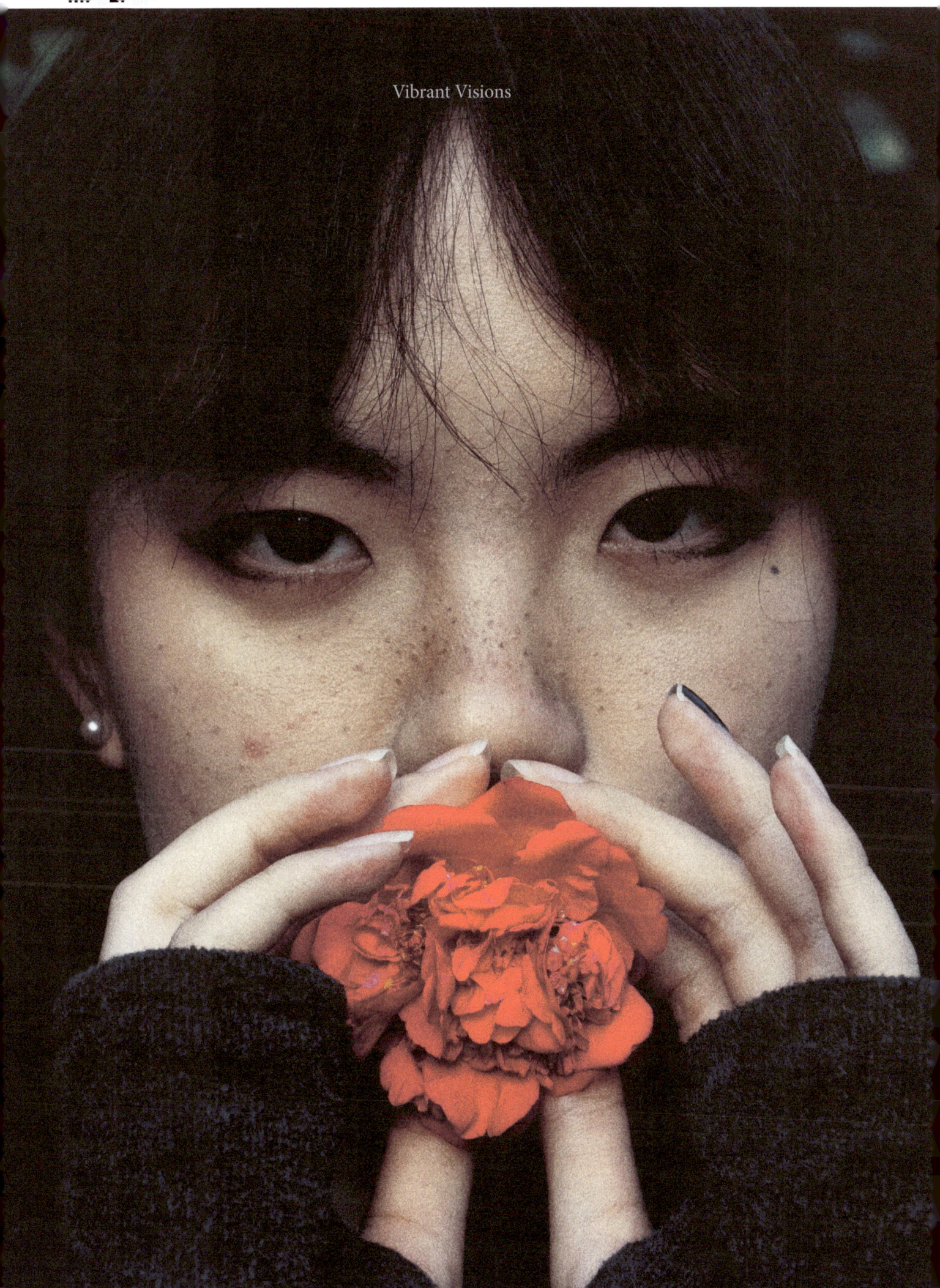
Vibrant Visions

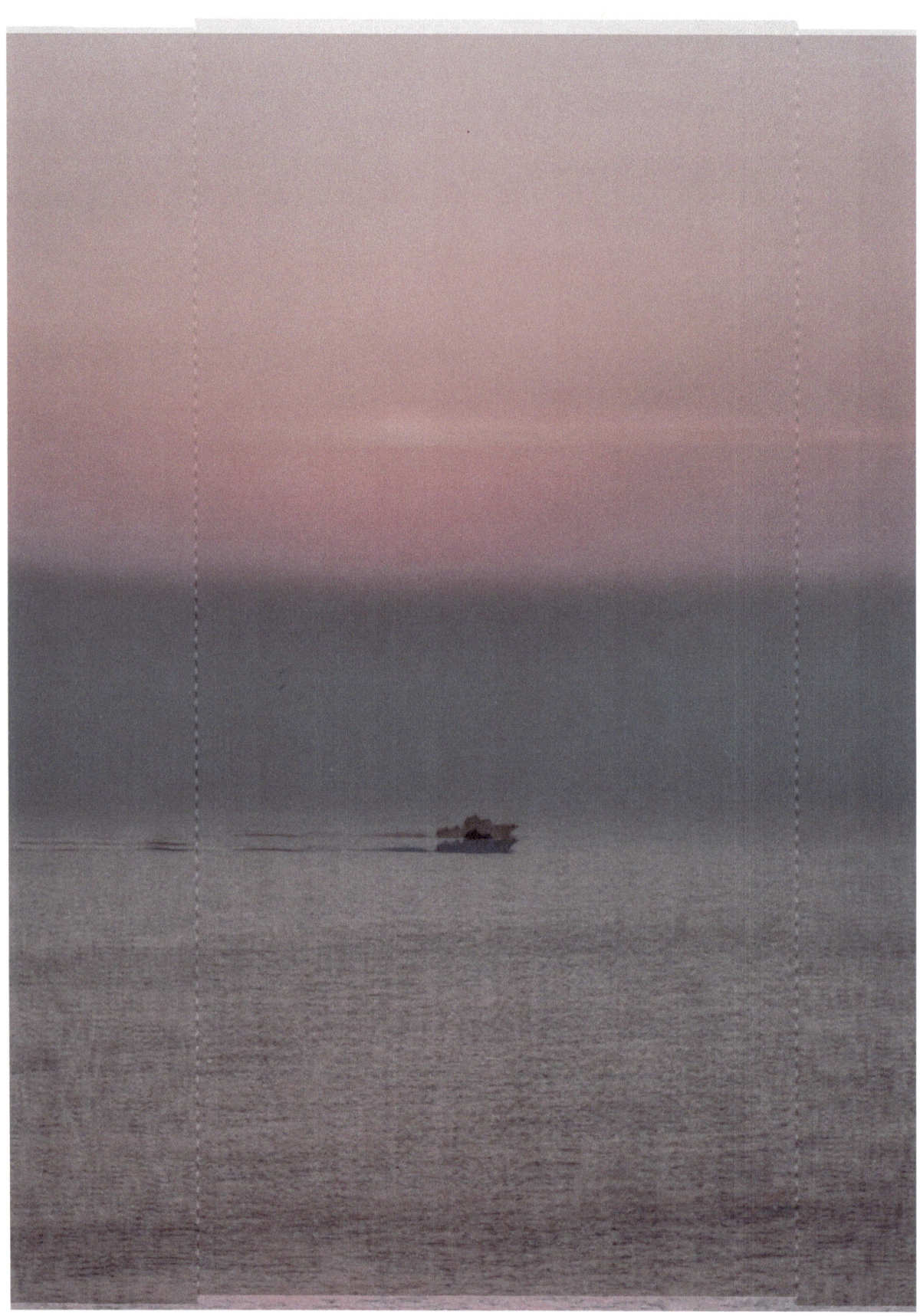

Walking on the Sea, photography

Vibrant Visions

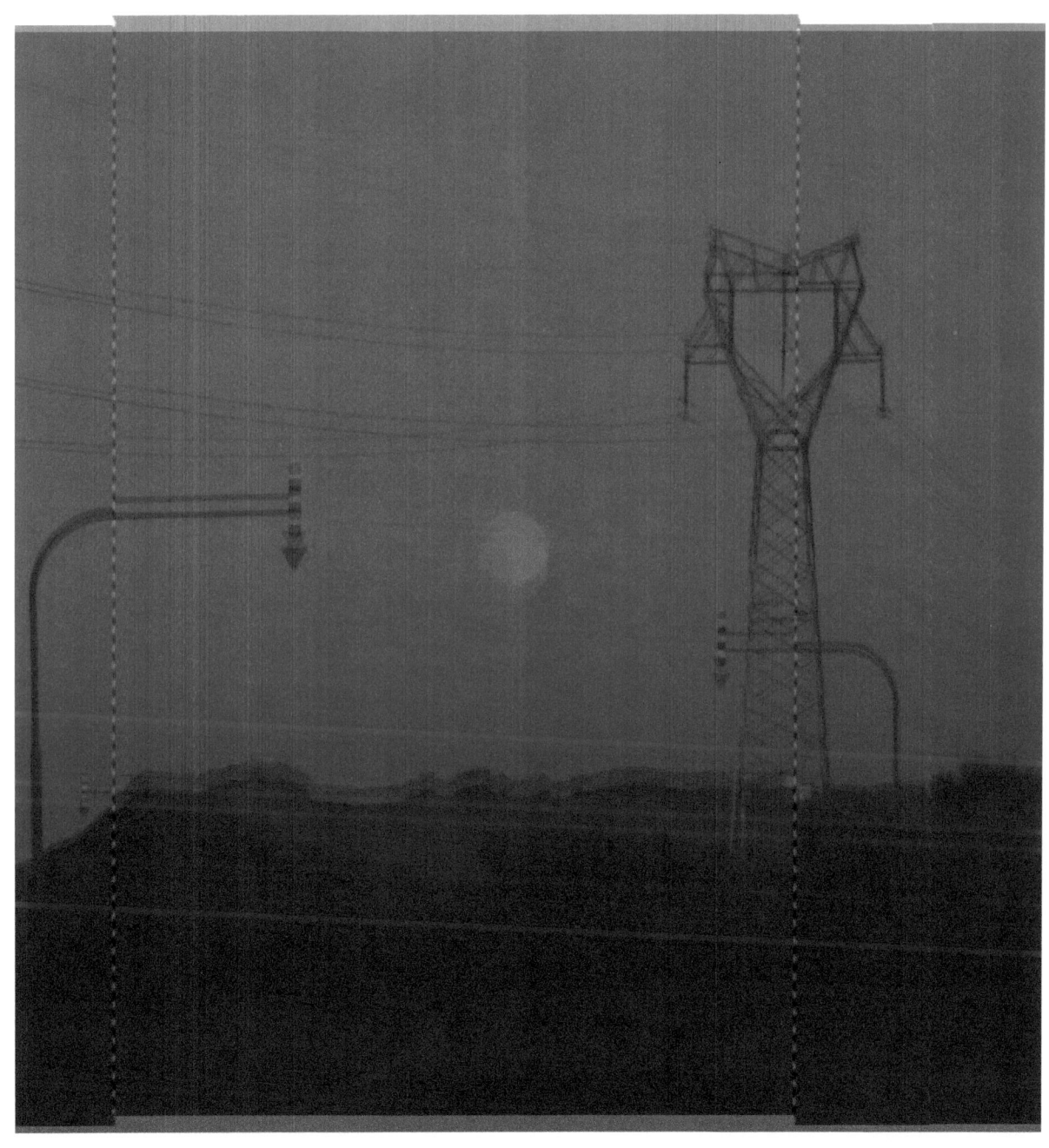

Please Take Care of Me, photography

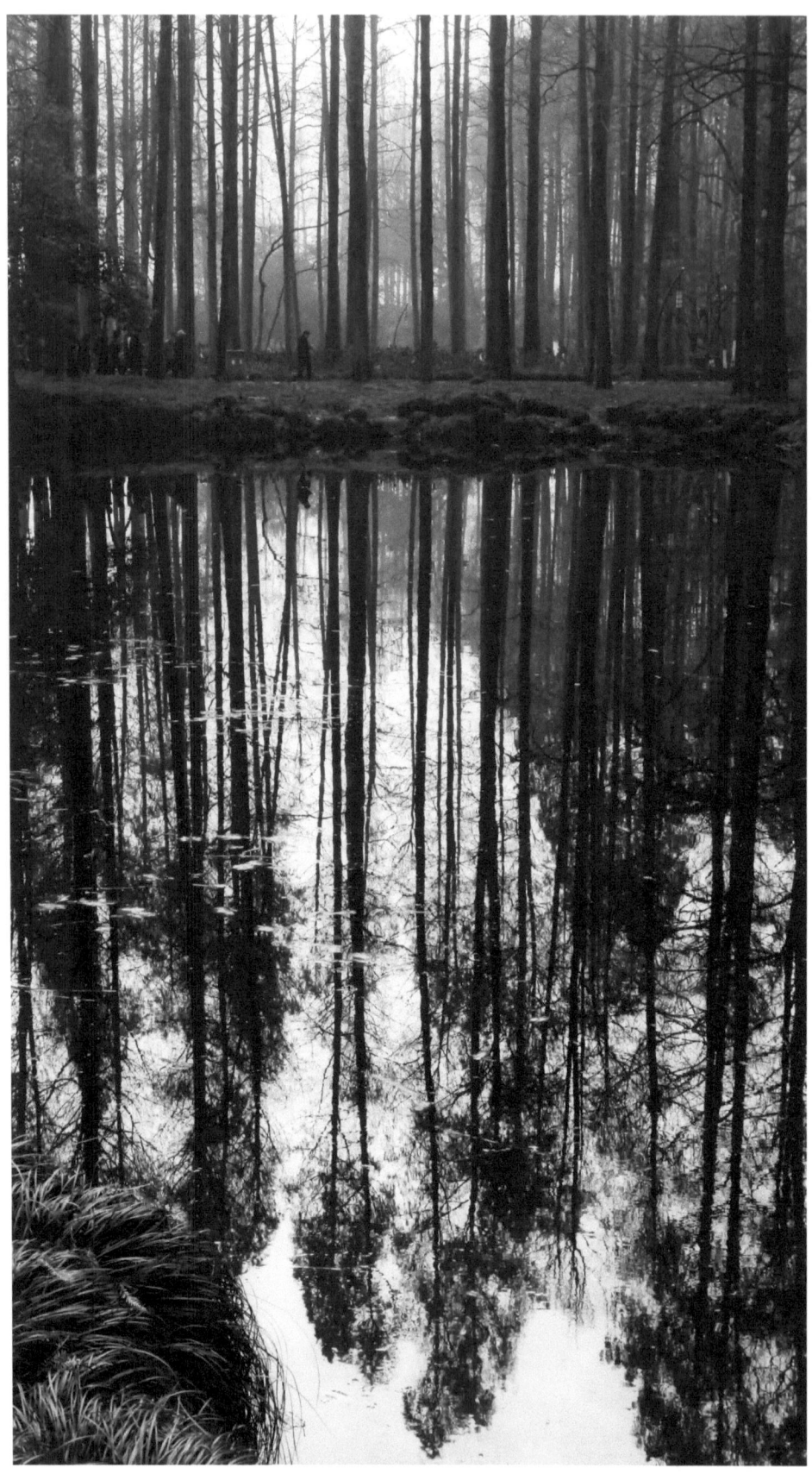

The Reflection of Nature, photography

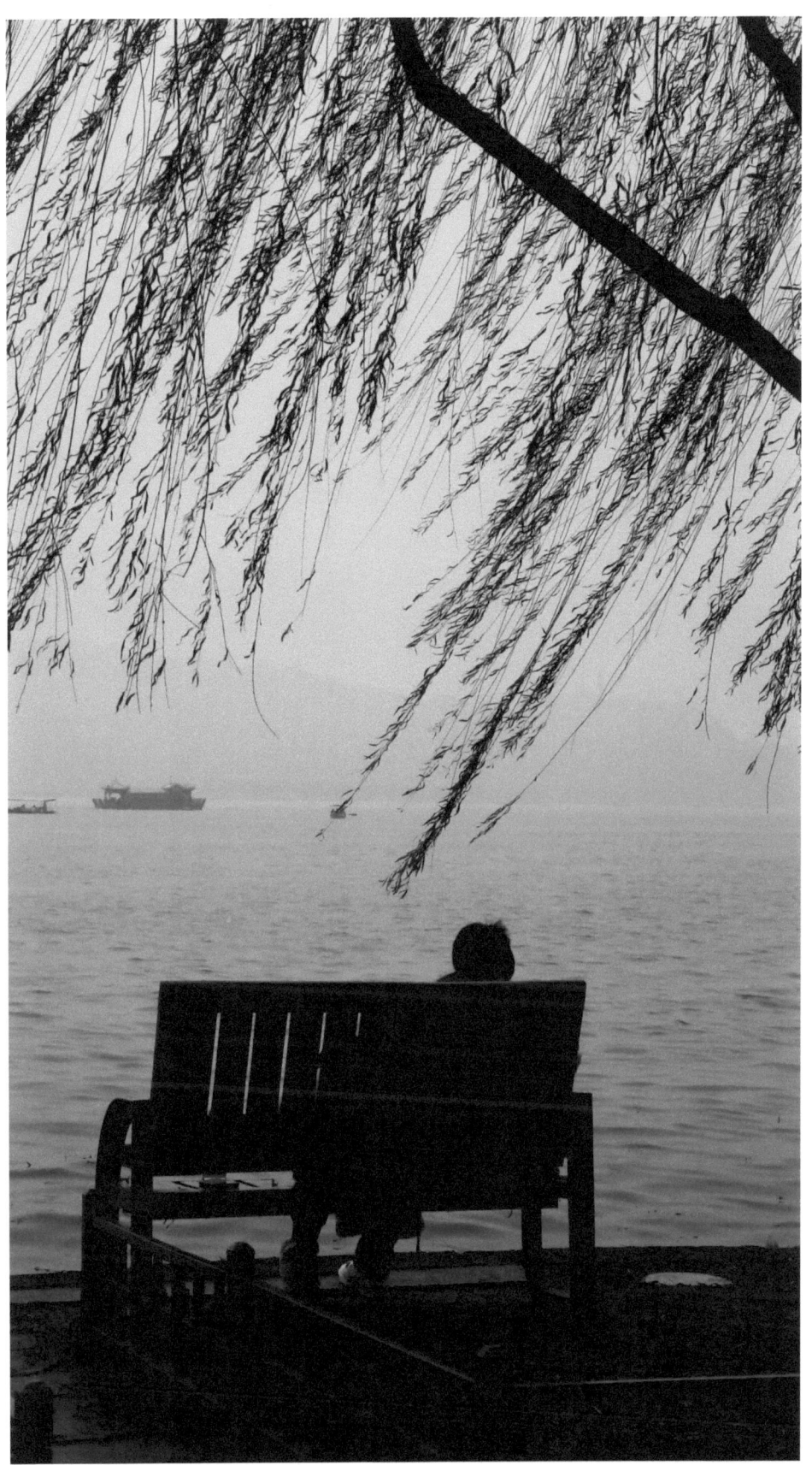

The Willow Watching the Sea, photography

The Kiss, photography

Vibrant Visions

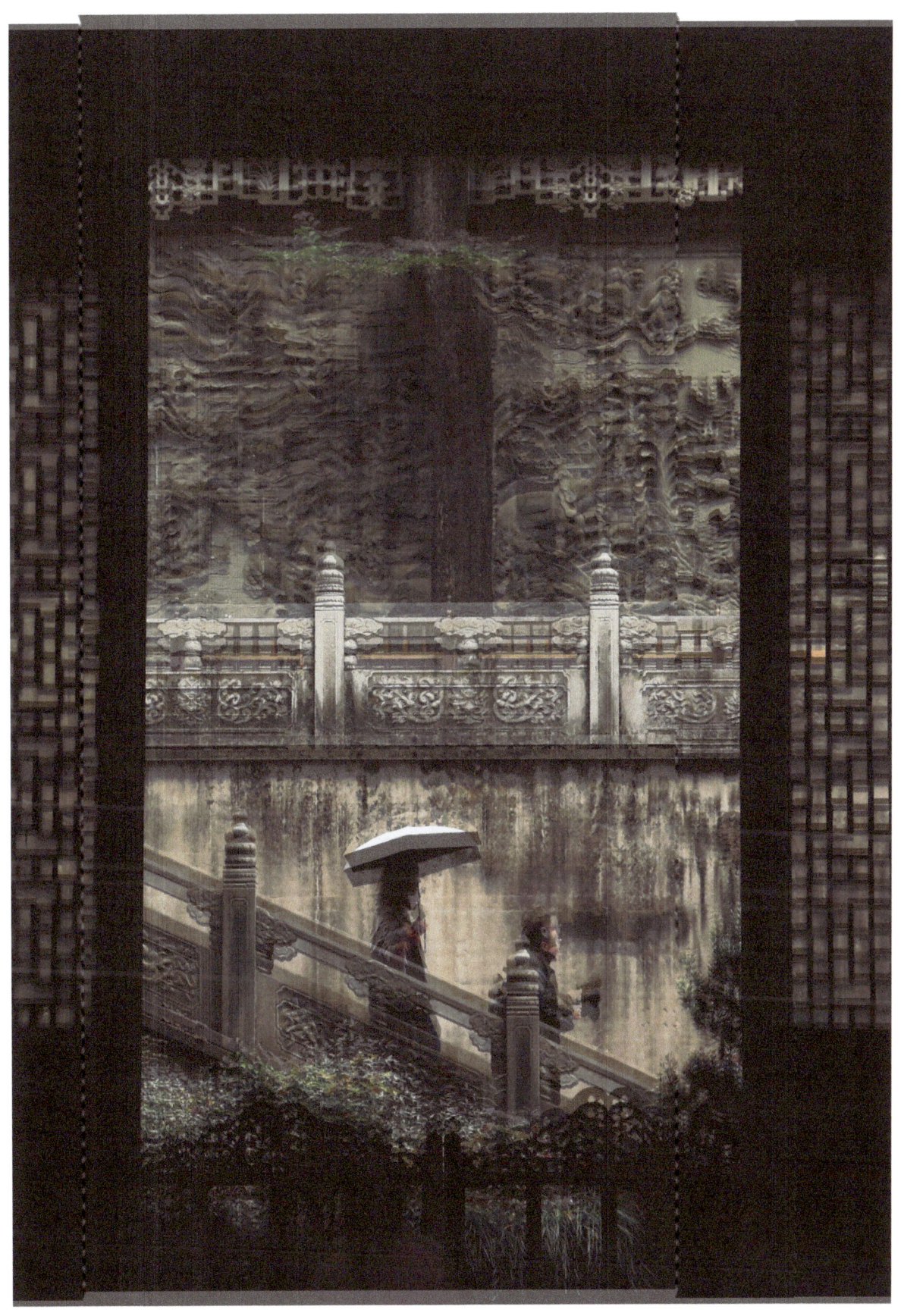

The Room Where Time is Visible, photography

YUIYAN WAN
Chino High School, USA

- **Silver Award for Art, 6th Liberty Awards, International Society of Young Artists, USA, 2023.**

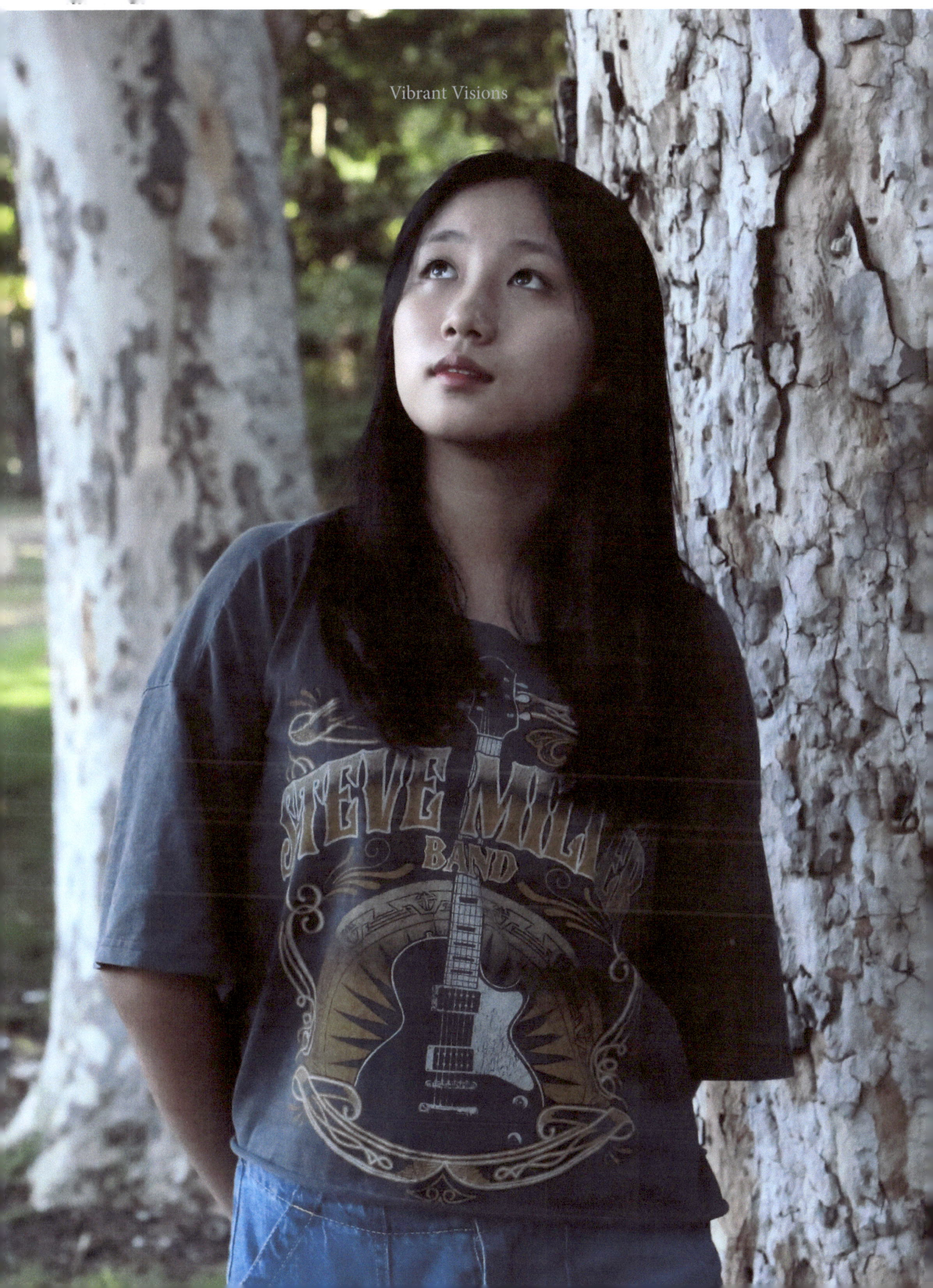
Vibrant Visions

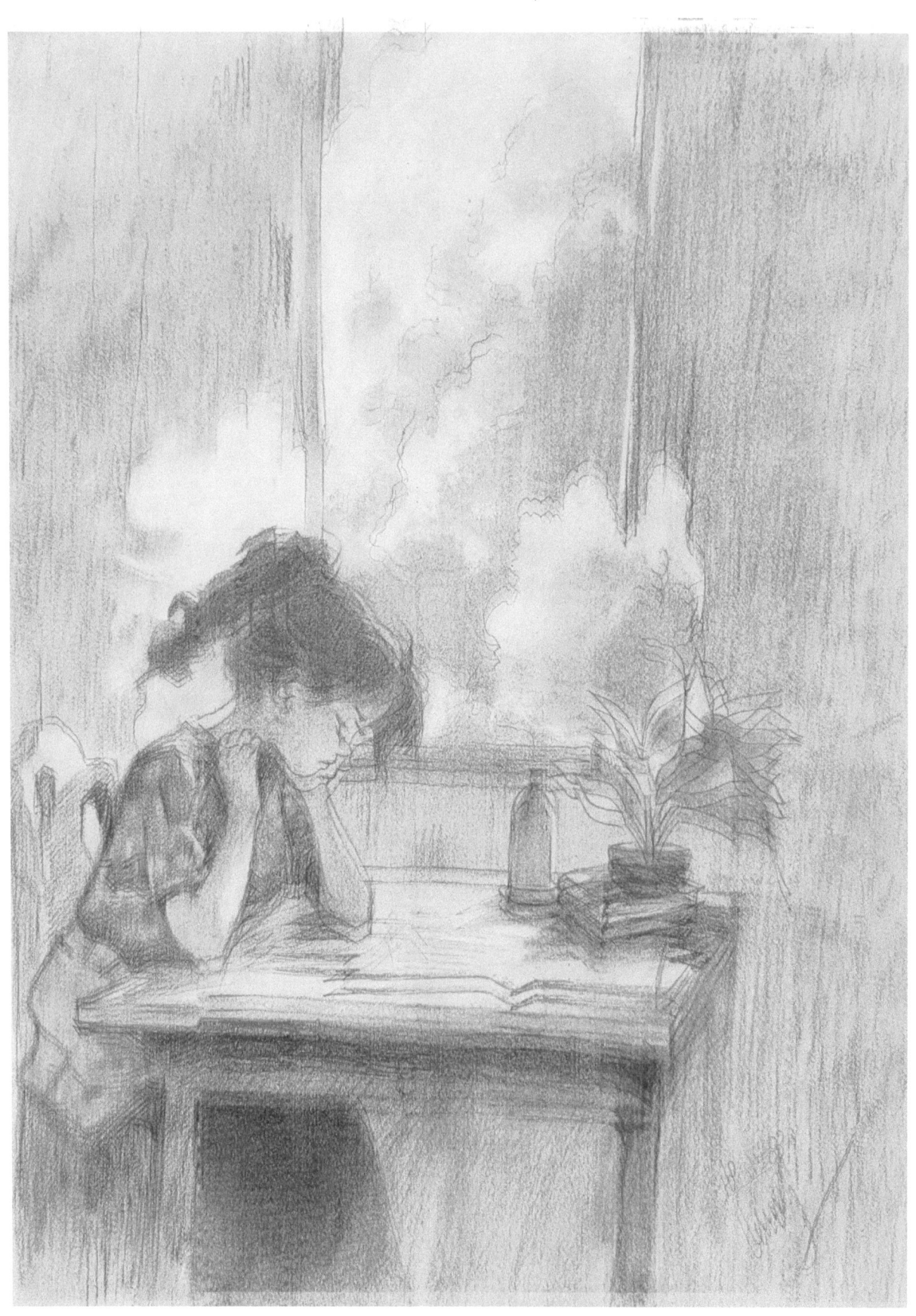

The Girl by the Window, pencil on paper

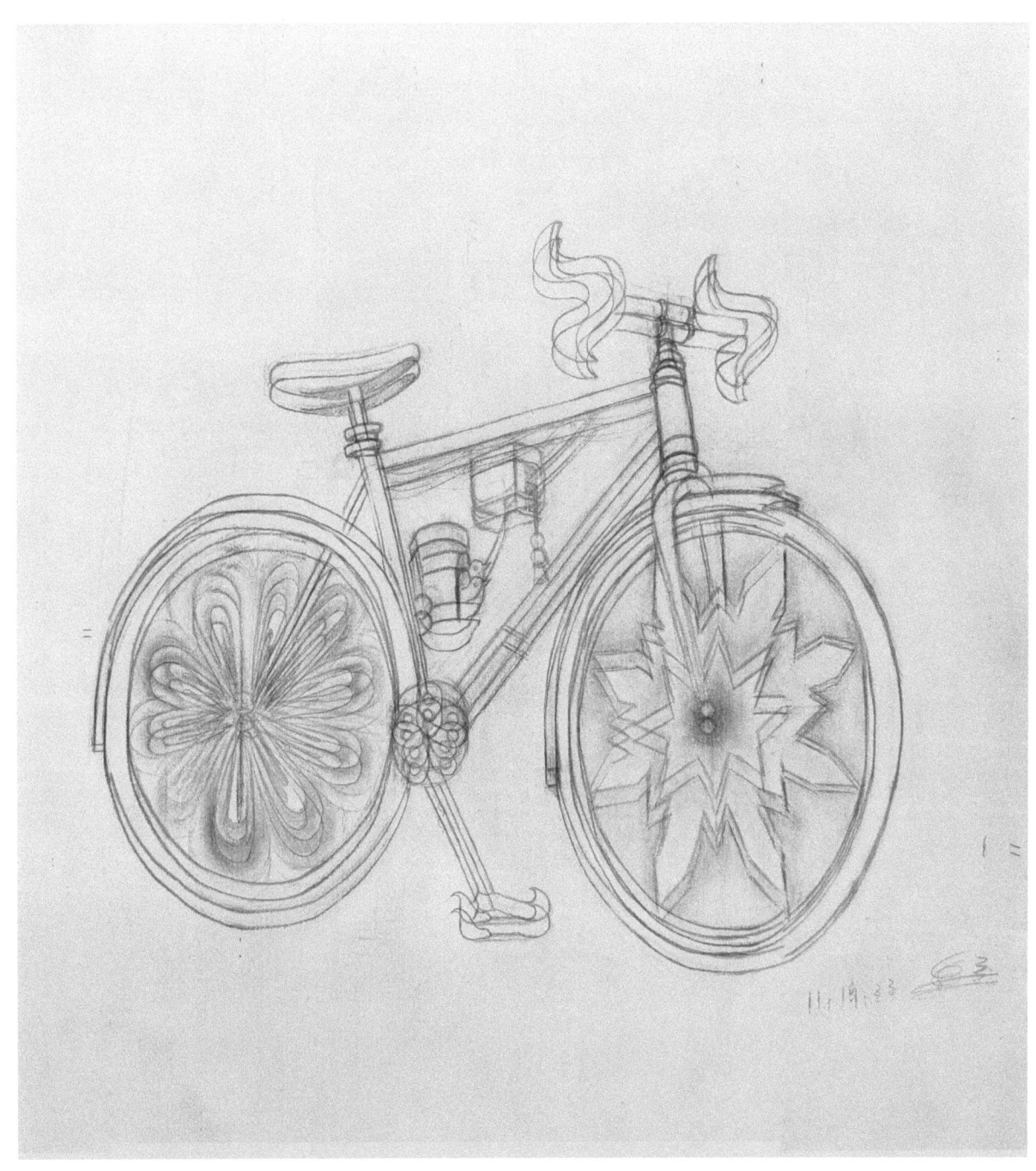

Bicycle Design Sketch, pencil on paper

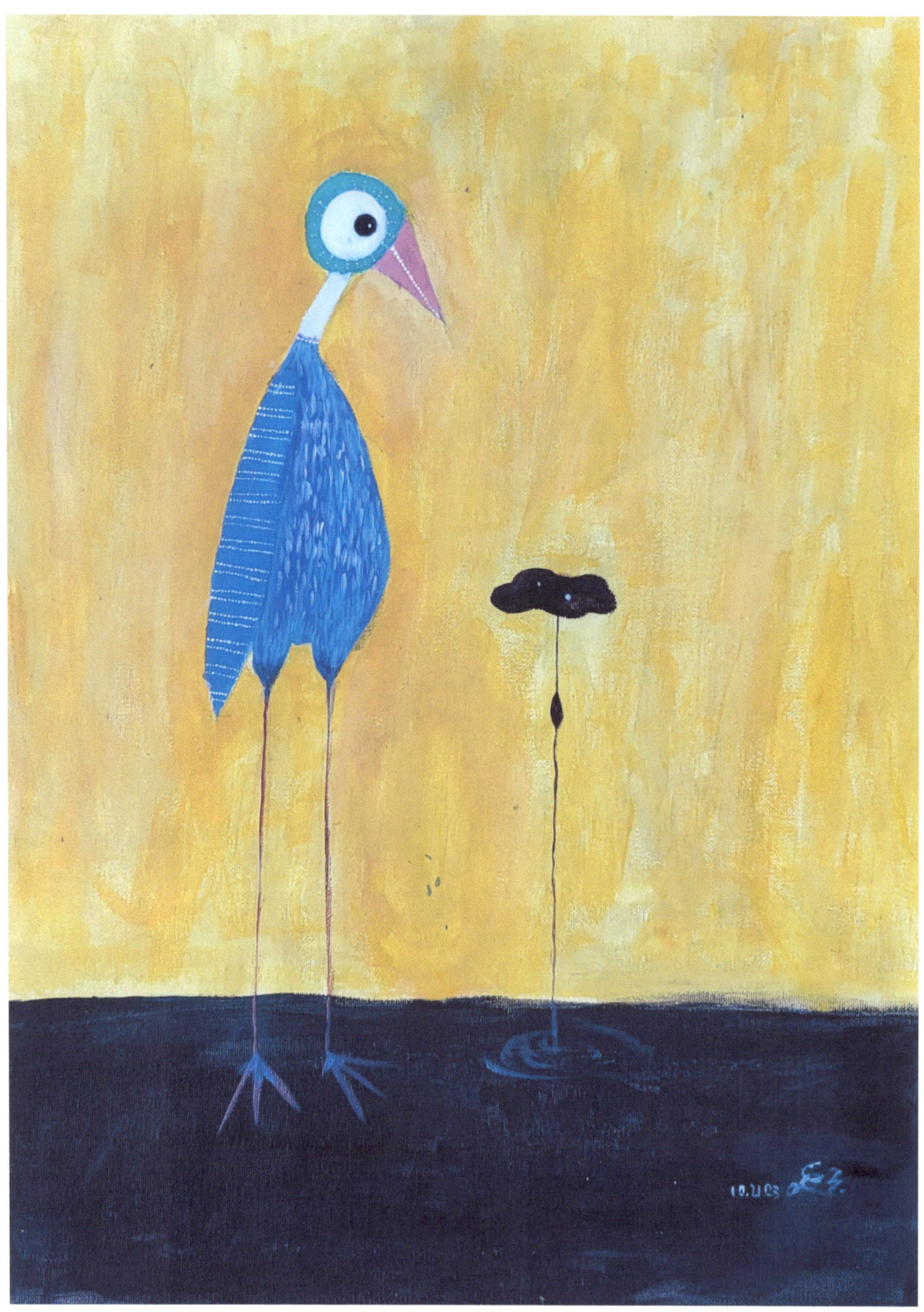

A Bird and a Lotus Flower, acrylic on Canvas

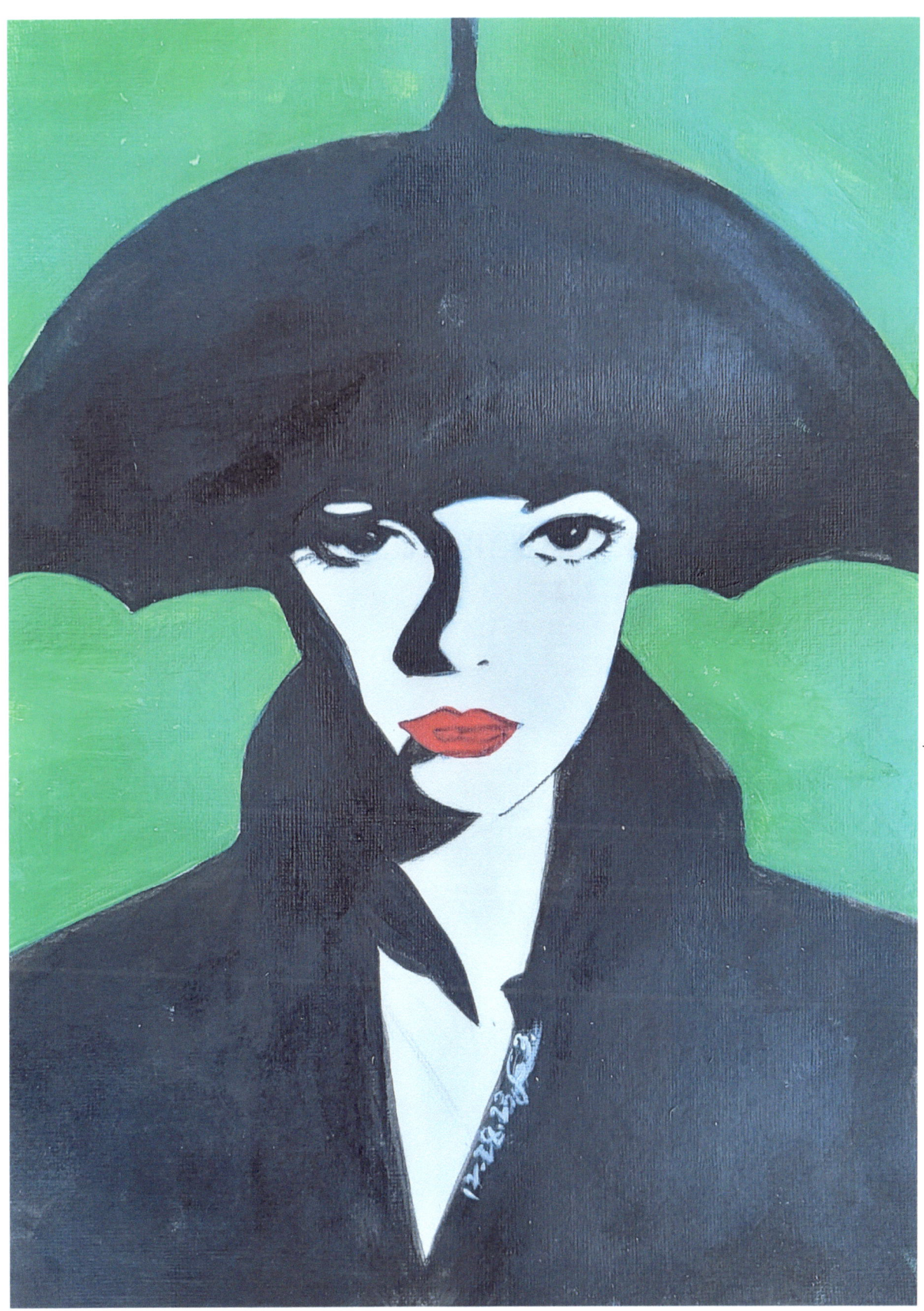

A Woman with an Umbrella, acrylic on Canvas

XIYU ZHANG
Qingdao Blue Valley Primary School, China

- Bronze Award for Art, 6th Liberty Awards, International Society of Young Artists, USA, 2023.

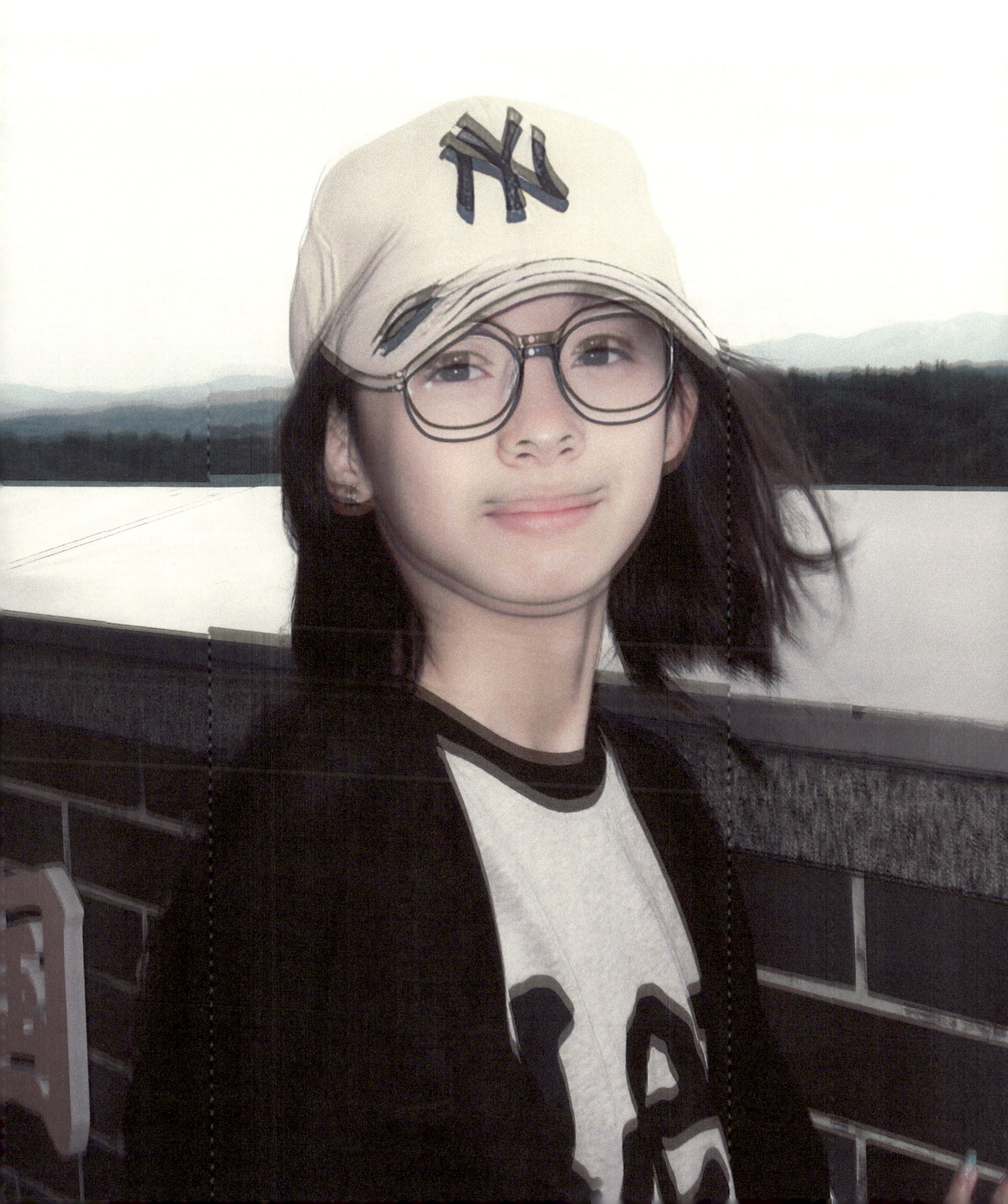

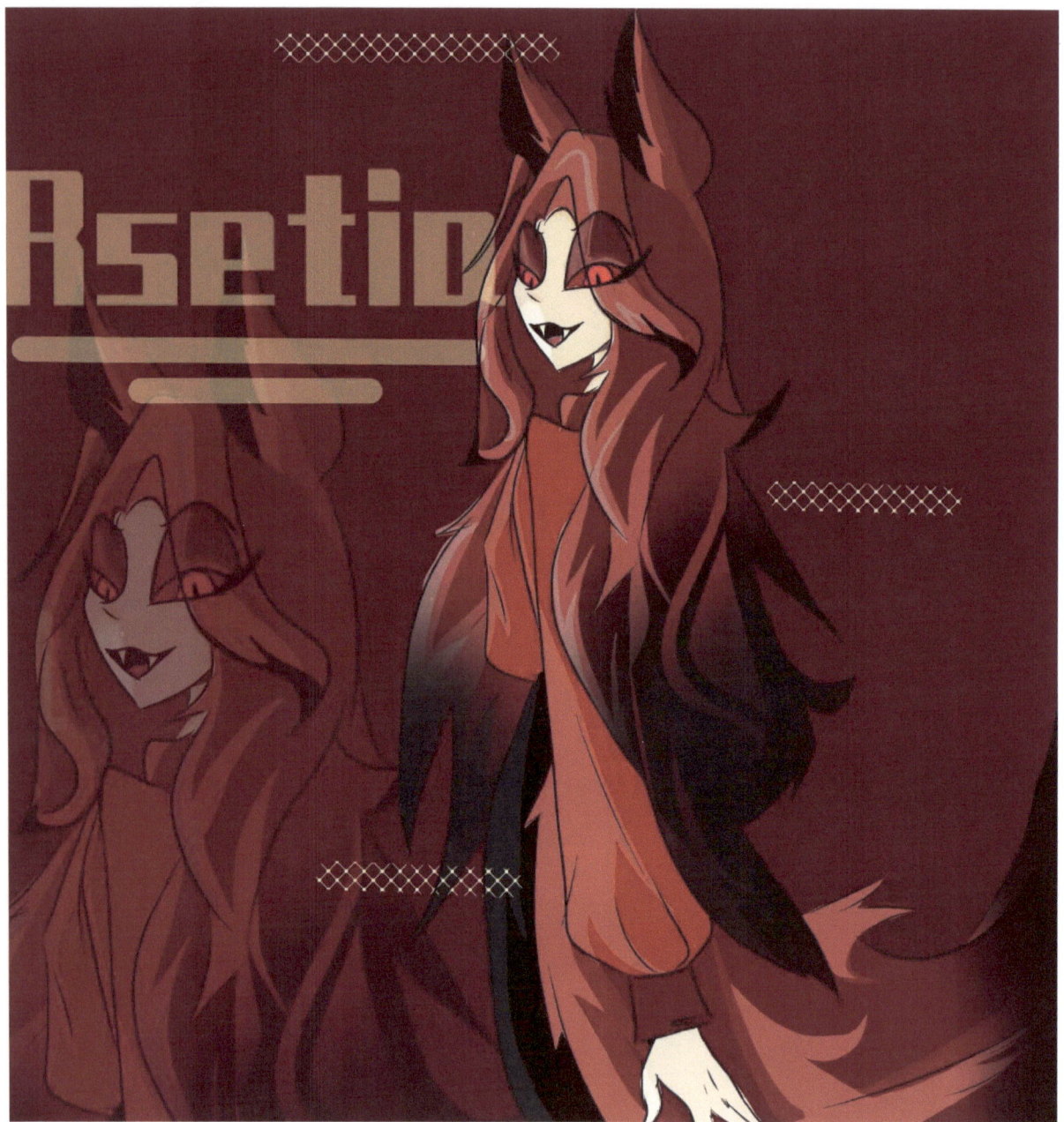

Rsetia, digital

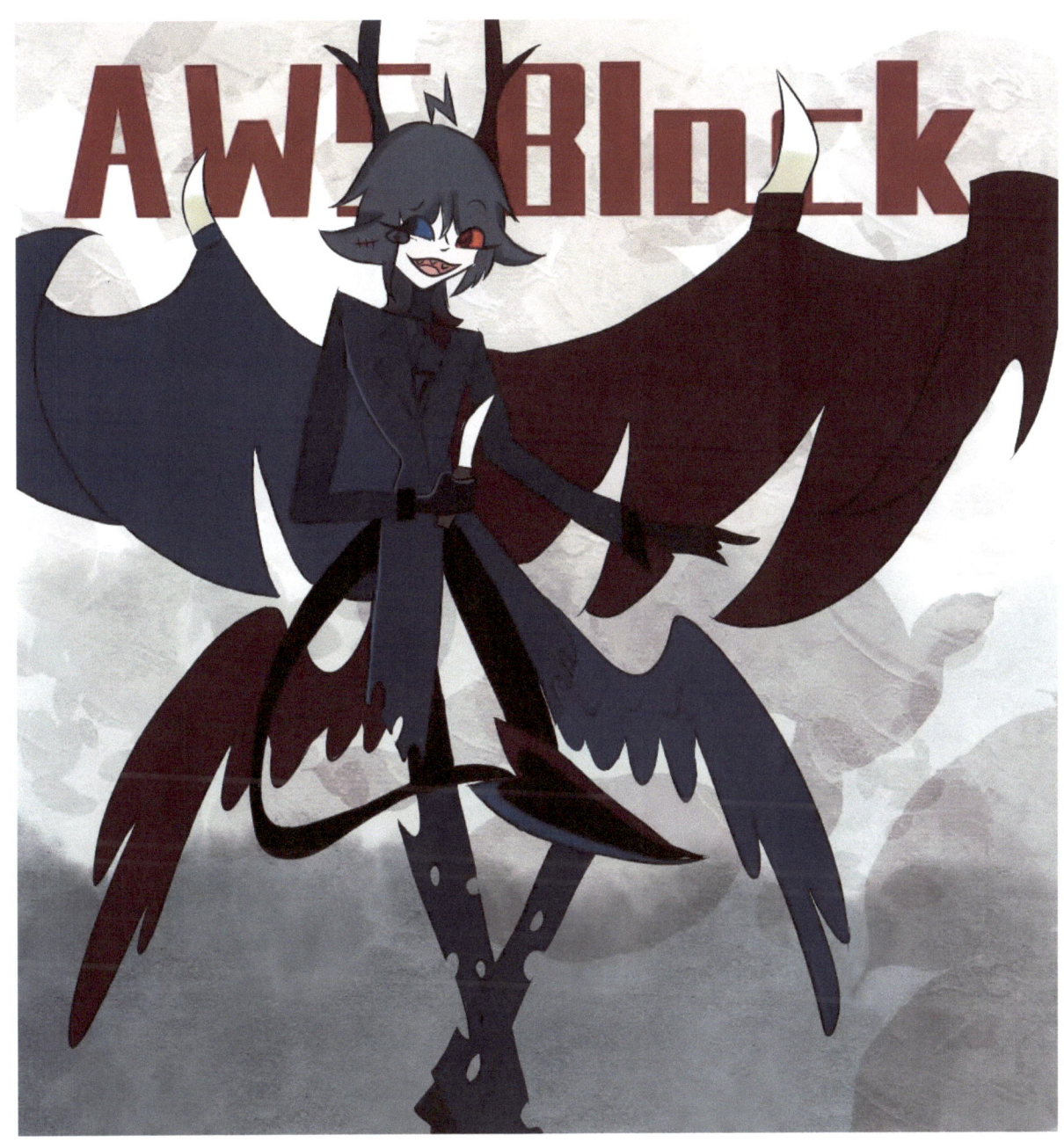

AWS. Black with a Dagger, digital

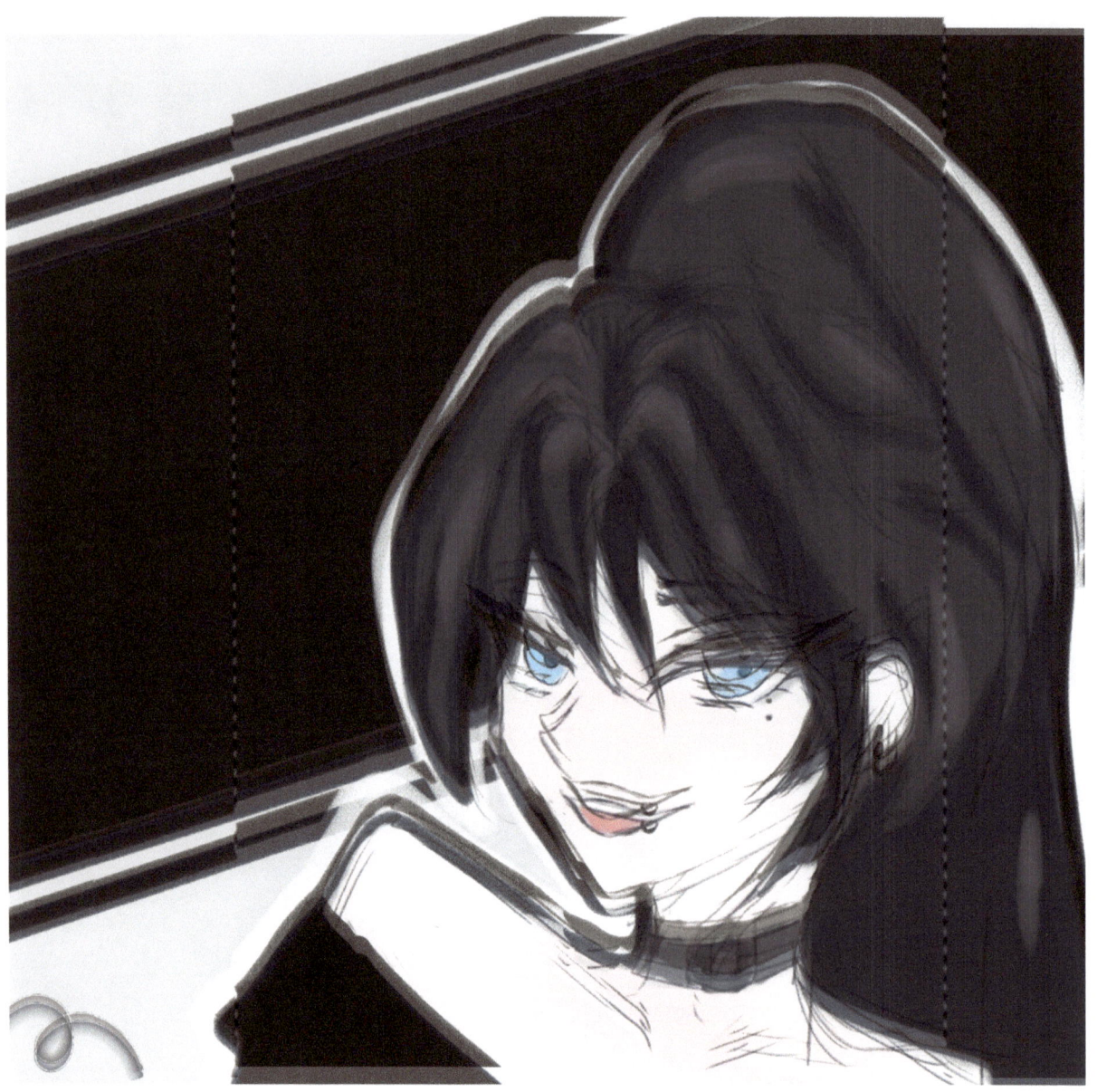

Melantha, digital

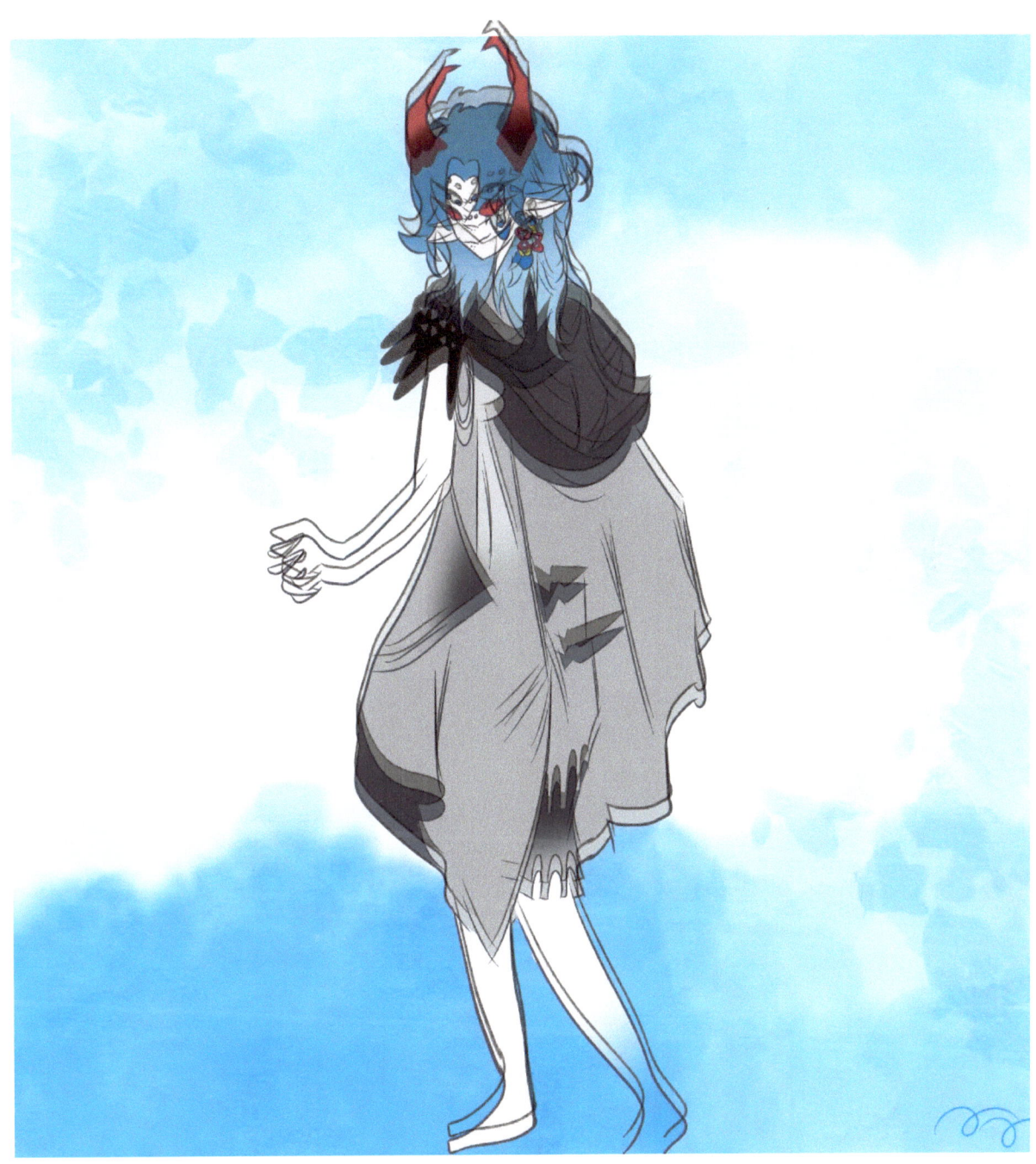

Avi, digital

YIHAN HU
Qingdao Chaoyin Elementary School, China.

- **Bronze Award for Art, 6th Liberty Awards, International Society of Young Artists, USA, 2023.**

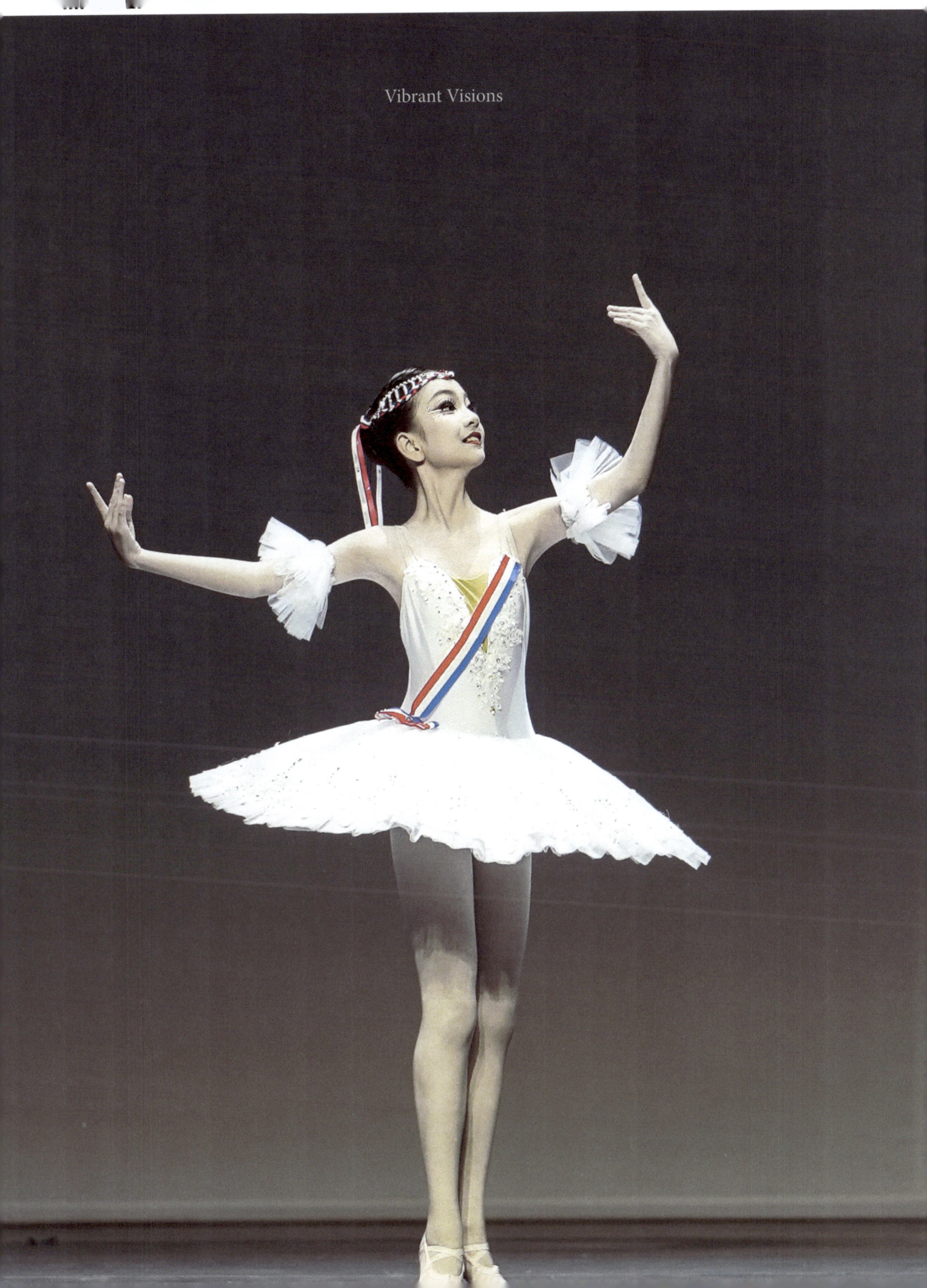

Vibrant Visions

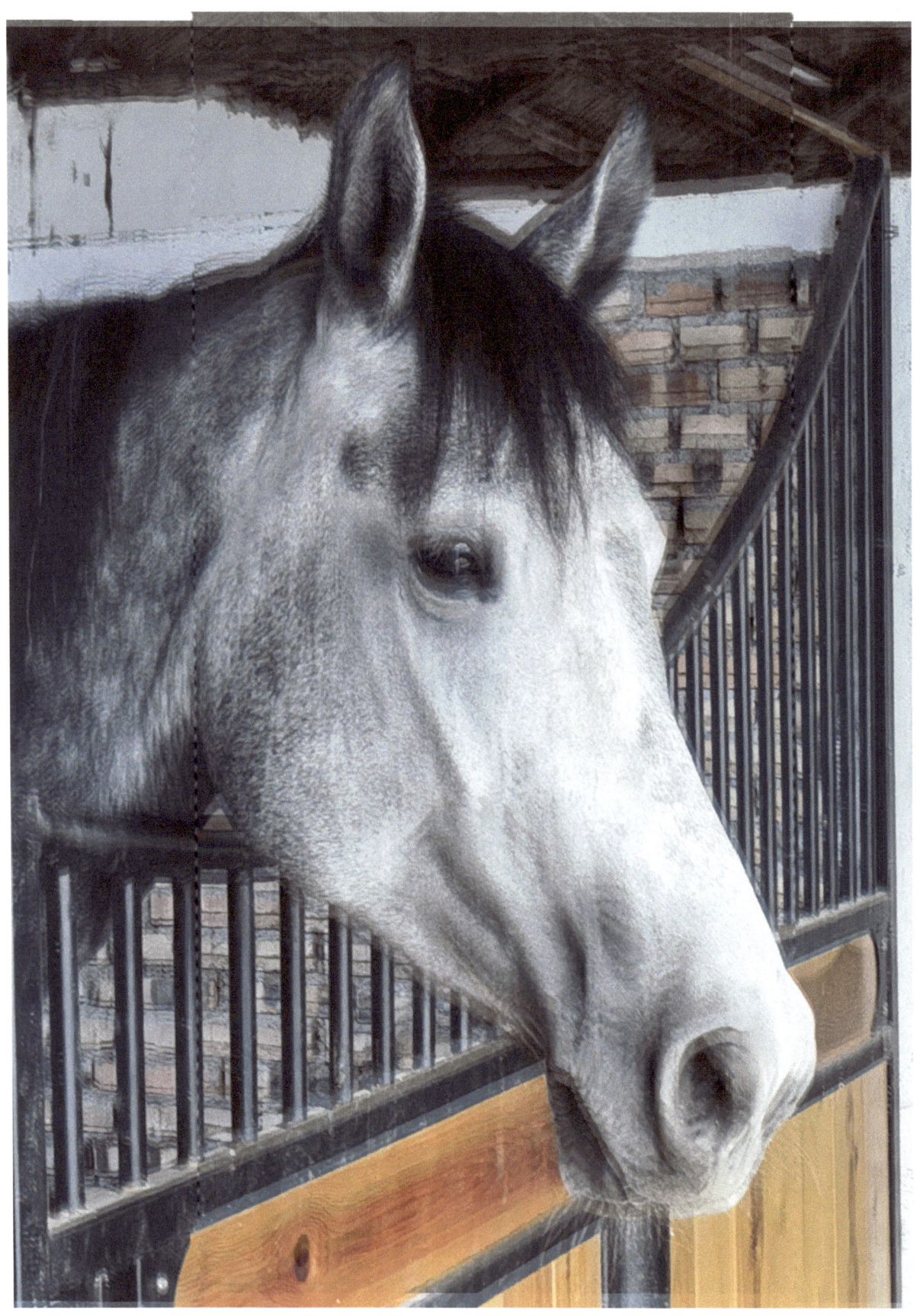

A Horse in the Stable, photography

Vibrant Visions

A Silver Dish, photography

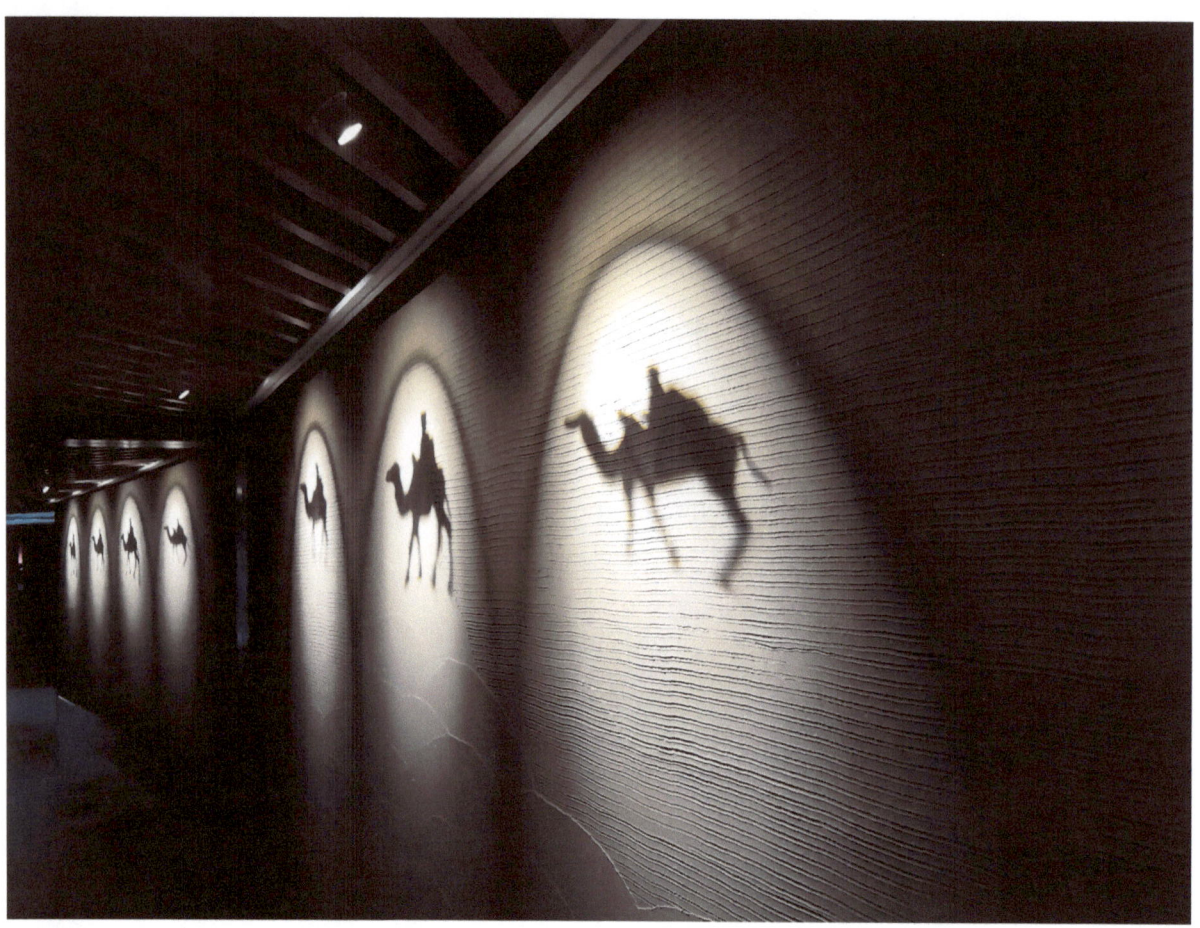

A Caravan of Camels on the Wall, photography

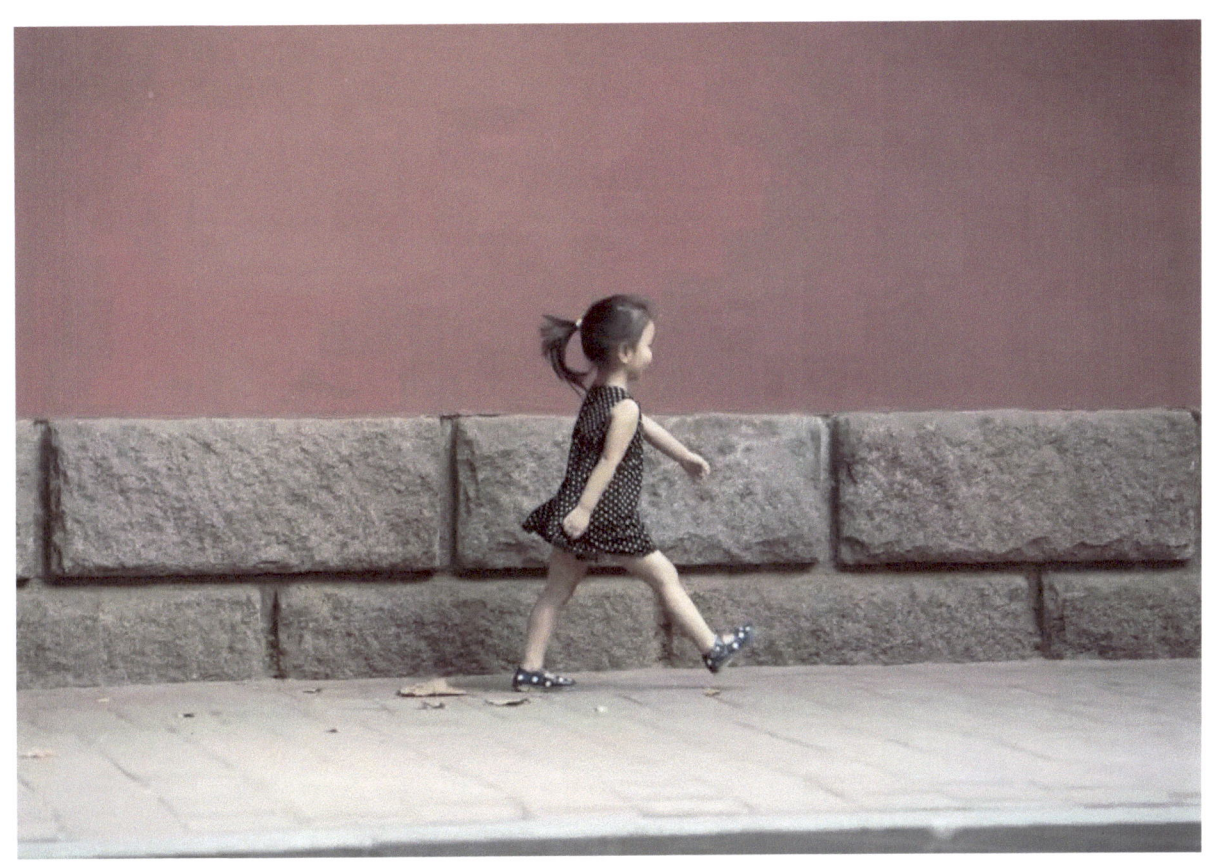

The Red Wall, photography

EMMA CHEN
Collingwood School, Canada

- Silver Award for Art, 6th Liberty Awards, International Society of Young Artists, USA, 2023.
- Silver Award for Art, 5th Liberty Awards, International Society of Young Artists, USA, 2022.
- Excellence Award, Artopia Youth Society, Canada, 2022.

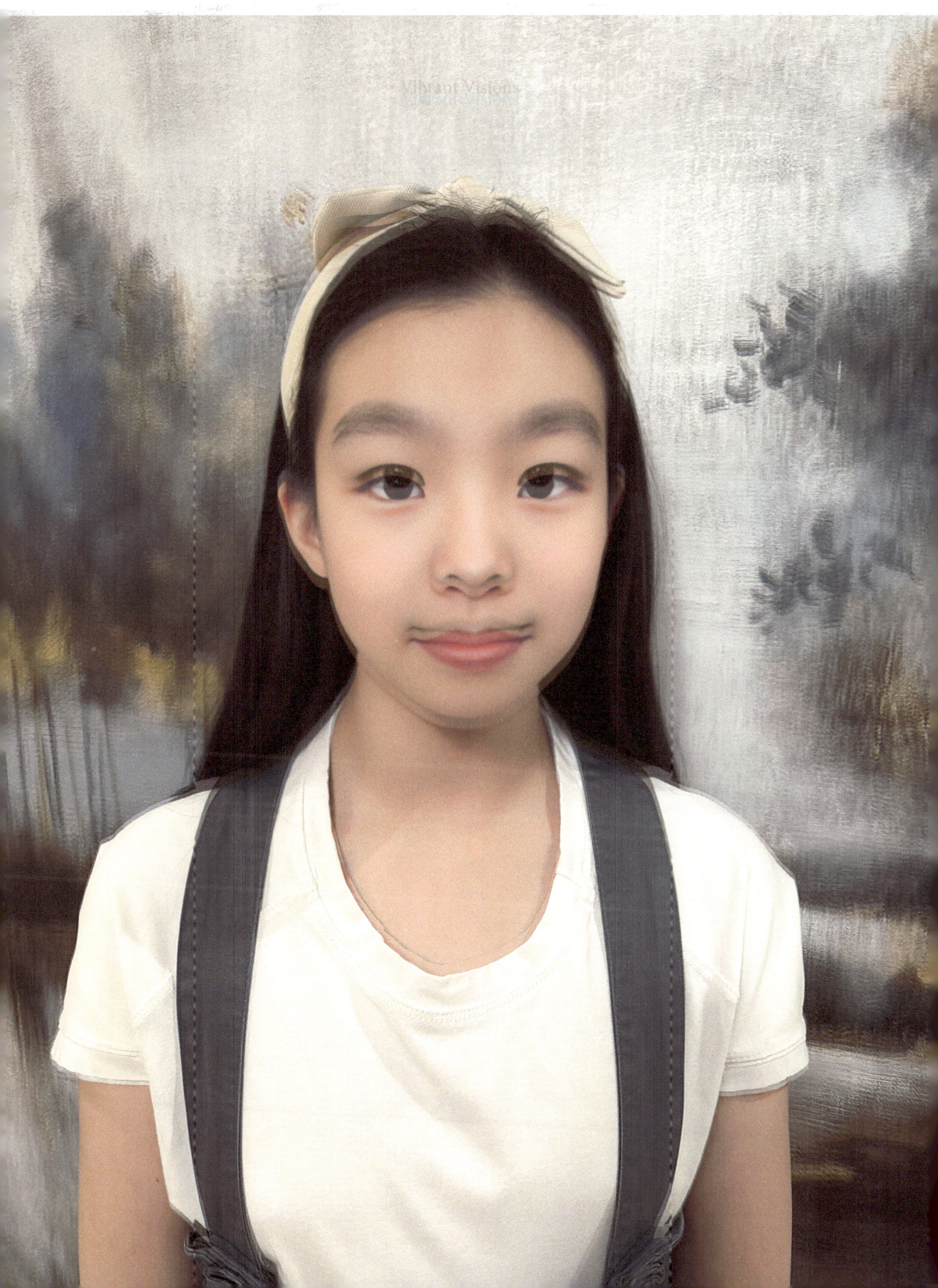

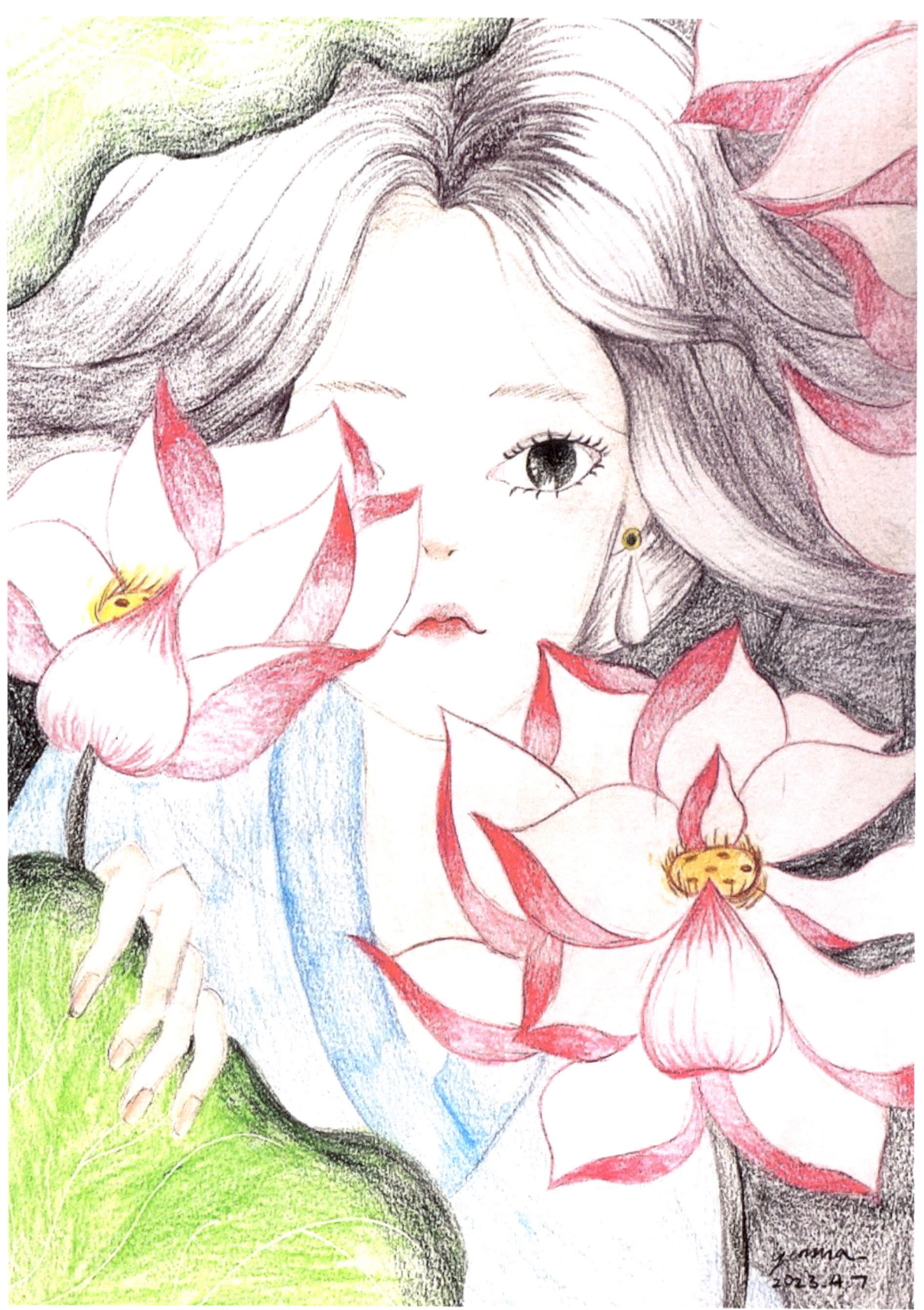

A Little Girl Among Flowers, acrylic on paper

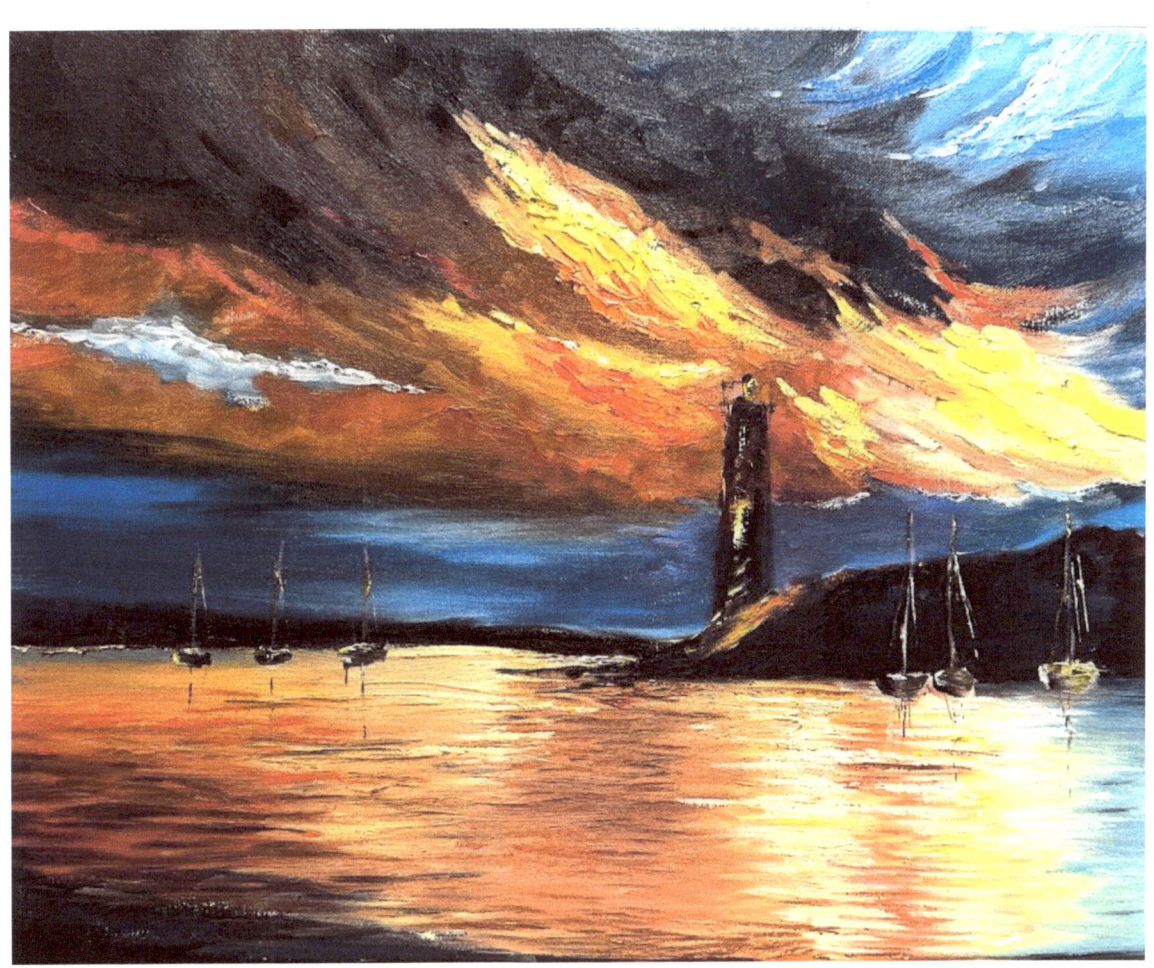

The Lighthouse, acrylic on paper

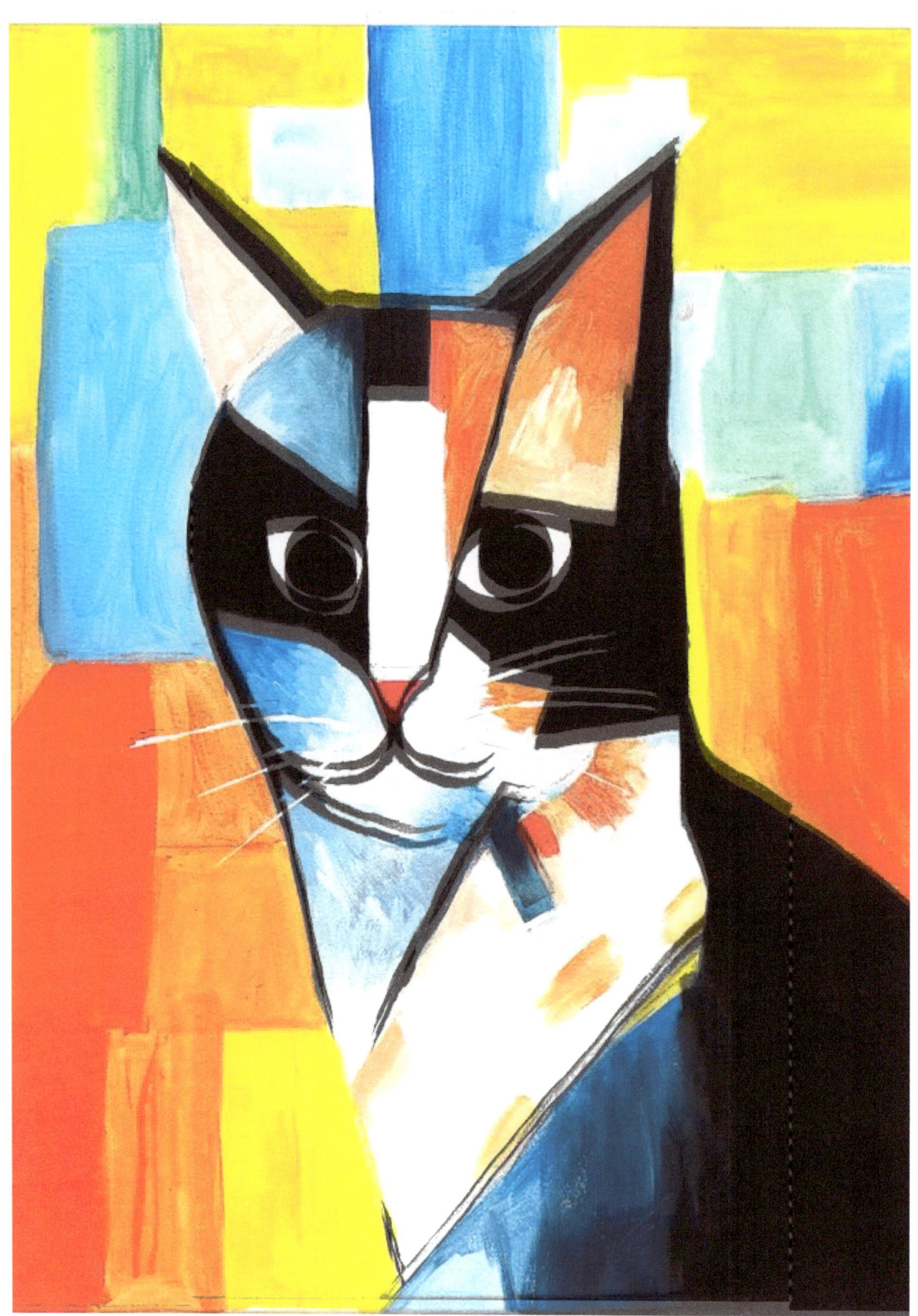

A Colorful Portrait of a Cat, gouache on paper

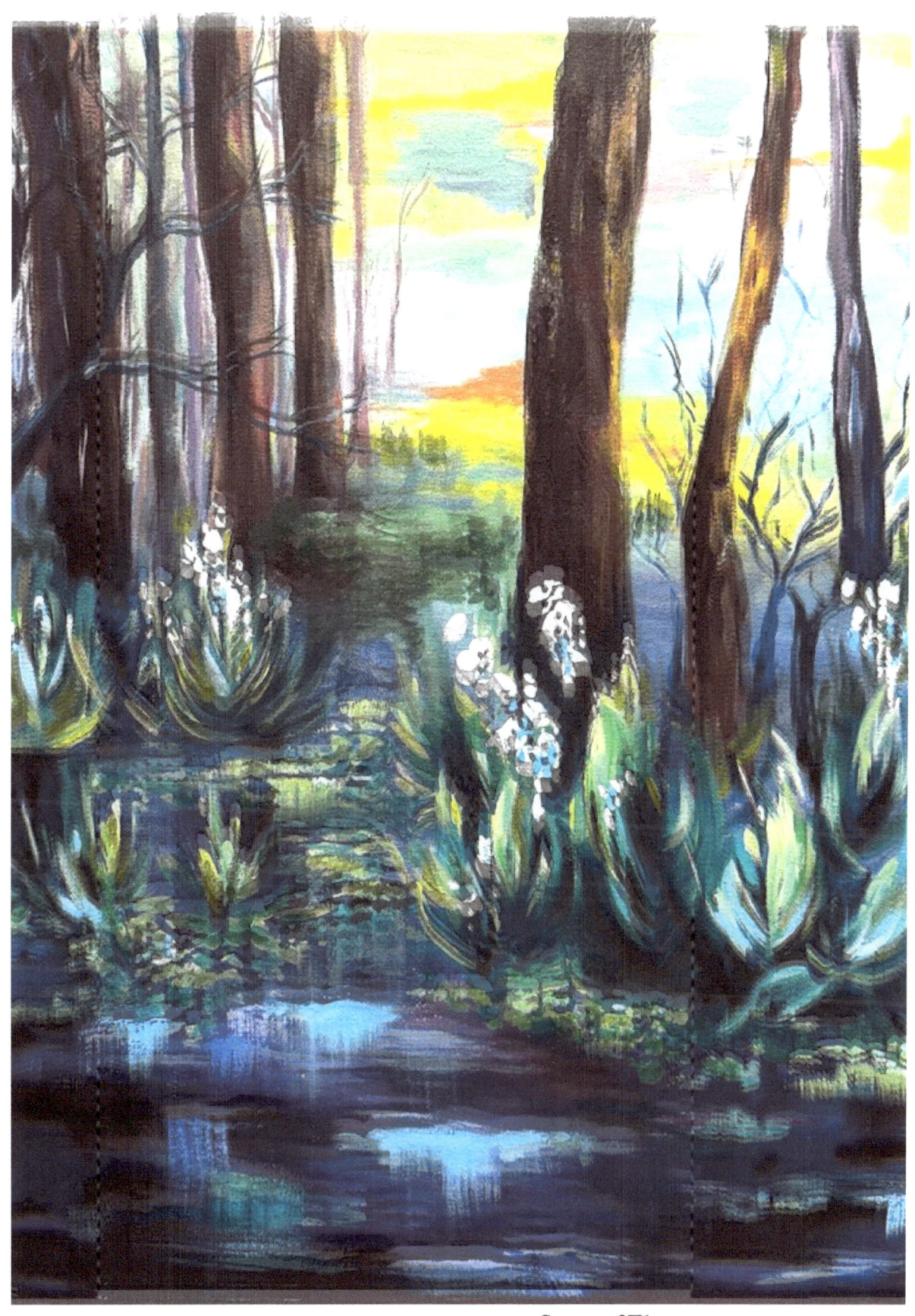

Scent of Flowers, paint pen on paper

The "Vibrant Future" International Education Project for Young Artists Publications List

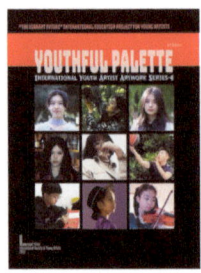

Youthful Palette: International Youth Artist Artwork Series-4, Los Angeles: Losget Press, 2023.

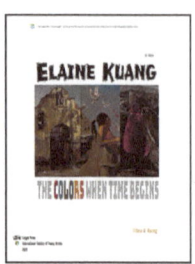

Elaine Kuang: The Colors When Time Begins, Los Angeles: Losget Press, 2022.

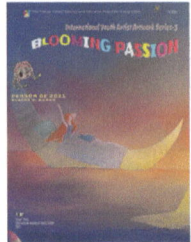

Blooming Passion: International Youth Artist Artwork Series-3, Los Angeles: Losget Press, 2022.

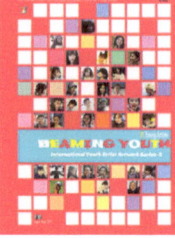

Beaming Youth: International Youth Artist Artwork Series-2, Los Angeles: Losget Press, 2021.

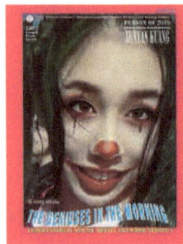

The Geniuses in the Morning: International Youth Artist Artwork Series-1, Los Angeles: Losget Press, 2020.

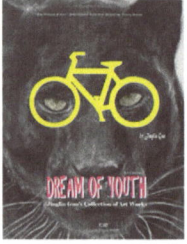

Dream of Youth, Los Angeles: Losget Press, 2019.

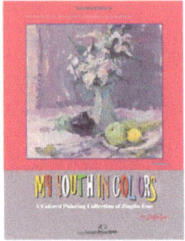

My Youth in Colors, Los Angeles: Losget Press, 2019.

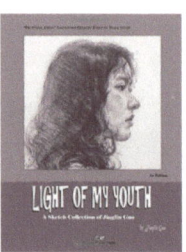

Light of My Youth. Losget Press, 2019.

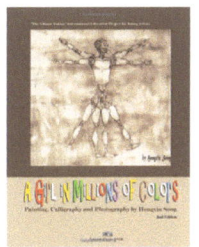

A Girl in Millions of Colors, Los Angeles: Losget Press, 2019.

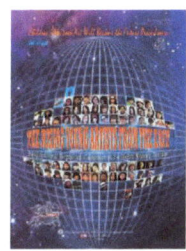

The Rising Young Artists from the East, Los Angeles: Losget Press, 2019.

The Young Picture Book Artists Program Publications List

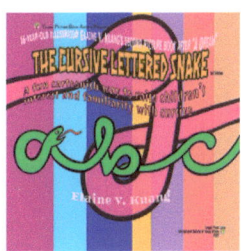

The Cursive Lettered Snake, Los Angeles: Losget Press, 2022.

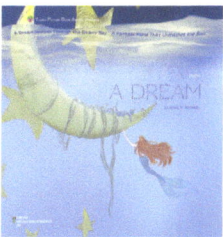

A Dream, Los Angeles: Losget Press, 2022.

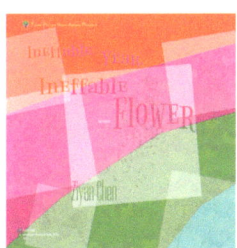

Ineffable Year, Ineffable Flower, Los Angeles: Losget Press, 2022.

International Youth Artist Artwork Series-5

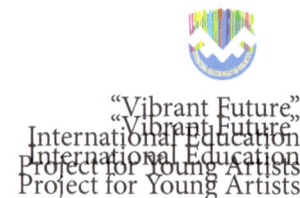

"Vibrant Future"
International Education
Project for Young Artists

Artists: Elaine V. Kuang, Jiajun Deng, Ziyan Chen, Rong Hong, Lujia Gao, Yuiyan Wan, Xiyu Zhang, Yihan Hu, Emma Chen
Editor-in-Chief: Yemen Chen
Deputy Editor-in-Chief: Jia Zhong
Editors: Elaine V. Kuang, Jiajun Deng
Cover designer: Jiajun Deng
Book designer: Jiajun Deng
Cover Artwork by: Ziyan Chen

 Copyright © 2024 by International Society of Young Artists
All rights reserved.

 Published in the United States by Losget Press, Los Angeles.
Originally published in paperback in the United States by Losget Press, in 2024.
Library of Congress Cataloging-in-Publication Data
Names: Kuang, Elaine V./ Deng, Jiajun/ Chen, Ziyan/ Hong, Rong/ Gao, Lujia/ Wan, Yuiyan/ Hu, Yihan/ Chen, Emma, authors.
Title: Vibrant Visions: International Youth Artist Artwork Series-5
Description: First edition. | Los Angeles: Losget Press, 2024.
Identifiers: LCCN 2824812884/ ISBN: 978-1-951364-40-3
E-mail: losgetpress@gmail.com
First printing: 2024.

www.ingramcontent.com/pod-product-compliance
Lightning Source LLC
Chambersburg PA
CBHW051916210526
45473CB00006B/2035